Hidden 7

CU00869244

By Anja Barker

A story about friendship and believing in yourself!

Contents

Chapter 1 – An art project gone wrong

It was only a few minutes before the school bell would ring, when my art teacher Miss Gosh walked over to my desk.

"What? This is by far the most ridiculous, disgusting thing I have ever seen! This is not a piece of art. This is simply absurd. What were you thinking? This just proves that you, Izzy Lane, have undoubtedly no talent or creative streak. No talent at all. I would suggest that, when you have finally grown up, you never, ever do anything that involves using your hands".

Wham, Bang. No messing about. Straight to the point! My rather angry art teacher Miss Gosh didn't just utter these words. Neither did she write them down calmly on a piece of paper. Nor did she decide to simply put her negative views in my next school report. That would have been tolerable. I could have coped with that. No. She had to yell those horrible words at me. Her chubby and plump face turning bright red and the wrinkles around her mouth popping out, as she shouted those horrible words at me. Her chubby arms were flapping around like a big goose that was too fat to take off. And worst of all -she had to yell at me right in front of my classmates. She had to embarrass me in front of the people that didn't care much about me and who, in no doubt, would use this to make fun of me even more.

I know I should have known better. Miss Gosh was one of the oldest teachers at my school. It wasn't a big school at all and opinions about teachers travelled far and fast. I heard about her last year, when some of the older pupils shared stories of how unreasonable she had been in class. And that she never, ever smiled. She had a non-existent sense of humour. She always looked annoyed and cross with the world. And I honestly believe that she doesn't even like being a teacher. Anyway, I got a bit distracted here.

My art teacher Miss Gosh had just yelled at me and informed me with her bitter and croaky sounding voice that the end of year project I had been working on at home for the past few weeks was utter rubbish. And if yelling at me in disgust was not enough, she also had to insult me. Telling me that I should never contemplate ever to do anything that involves using my hands when I grow up. Mind you, at 10 years young, thinking about what I wanted to do when I was a grown-up was not something I had seriously thought about. So, I shouldn't really get too annoyed about that.

The second Miss Gosh had stopped yelling at me I could feel myself getting very angry. Obviously, I did not agree with her. I thought my art project was ingenious and totally creative. And I hate being yelled at. It was bad enough when my mother would yell at me for not having gotten dressed in time. Or for not having taken the rubbish out. But to be yelled at by a teacher was a different story. That caused a different kind of anger.

It started in the pit of my stomach. Deep inside me. It felt like a big, solid marble that moved from one side to the next. It made my stomach hurt. Then it moved up to my chest. Then my throat. Then my head. The marble wanted to come out. It wanted to jolt all the way over to Miss Gosh and hit her in the face. I could feel that my cheeks were getting hot and itchy. Another sign that I was getting very angry, indeed. I took a deep breath. And another one. Until I could feel the cold air filling my lungs, cooling me down from the inside. It has taken me the last 3 years to learn how to keep that big marble inside me. It was still hard. I took another breath and quietly counted to five. My mother always said that being angry is fine. As long as it is only in your head. No one likes an angry girl. Especially not my own mother, who taught me that being openly angry would only lead to a consequence. Like taking my i-pad away. Or making me go to bed early at 7pm. So, I took another deep breath and when I felt the big marble slowly rolling down back inside my stomach again, I quietly put down the paint brush I was holding and stared into Miss Gosh's dull grey eyes. And then I did what I do best. The thing I knew was going to work. It always worked with adults. I didn't need to use my hands for this. I smiled. Well, I did not just smile. I gave her my biggest, cutest and most beaming smile, ever. I knew she had not expected that.

"I am sorry you feel that way Miss Gosh." I said in my most innocent sounding voice. Of course, that was not what I was thinking. I was not sorry at all. I had worked really hard on my "Moving monster creature" art project. I actually was quite proud of my own creativity. I didn't just want to do another one of those cardboard boxes that moves when you tap it. I wanted to create something special. Something that looked real. And in my defence Miss Gosh did not really explain to us what we could use and what we could not use. All Miss Gosh said was that it needed to be made by us and that we were only allowed to use things we found in our house.

As it happened, I found a big toy dinosaur skeleton in my little brother's room, which I sneaked out one night when he was fast asleep. I was sure that he wouldn't notice. His room was full of toys and I hadn't seen him play with it for many weeks. I then found a little toy bird in our playroom and with the help of some string, lettuce leaves and some ketchup created a "Bird eating dinosaur monster". I agree that by the time my creation was finished, the salad leaves had turned a weird brownish colour and the ketchup developed a funny smell. But nonetheless, judging by all the other boring moving creatures in my class, mine not only looked like a real monster but it also smelled like one. In my eyes that deserved admiration and a round of applause. Not some unjustified yelling and shouting from my teacher.

To my relief the school bell rung just as Miss Gosh was about to say something in return. I kept smiling at her, took my school bag and then left my classroom for a well-deserved break.

Half-way down the corridor, I could see that my two classmates Dana and Christina were already waiting for me. I sighed. If only they could have just walked on instead of blocking the corridor, waiting to snigger some horrid comments at me. Something they did all the time. Both were best friends with each other. You never saw one without the other. They both went to the loo at the same time. They ate their lunch and snacks together. At breaktimes they would always hang out together. They even called each other in the morning to agree on what hair style they would wear that day. They bought the same school shoes and wore the same coat. Even though the school did not allow us to wear make-up, I swear that they wore mascara every single day. I called them the "Princess Twins". Not because they really were princesses. More because they acted like ones. They were spoilt, opinionated and vain. And expected everyone to just do whatever they wanted them to do. They decided who was cool and who was not.

Unfortunately for me, because I don't really like doing what people want me to do. I didn't care about my hair enough to make it look fancy. I chose clothes that felt good on my skin and not because they made me look good. And I certainly did not want to put some fake colour on my face. More often than not, I thought the Princess Twins' eyes looked like those of a Panda bear. I liked my eyes to look human. In short, I was not in their "magic circle" of friends and followers. Thankfully (because I knew when to keep my mouth shut) a lot of the time they simply ignored me. And I tried to ignore them. Sometimes I could overhear their conversations and what I heard made me cringe. They were not only opinionated but also rude and mean. Only last week they loudly discussed the size of Martha's legs and compared them to tree trunks. Everyone in their circle laughed about those comments. I thought they were simply nasty. I liked Martha, especially since she spent most of her time after school playing football. She was one of the fastest girls I knew. Maybe that's why the twins picked on her. They were jealous.

Anyway, today, though, after having been yelled at, I could see out of the corner of my eye that the Princess Twins would not ignore me. Today I would be the centre of their nastiness. Both looked at me with the sort of "We are going to make fun of you" look. I held on to my school bag, kept my eyes fixed on the floor whilst quickly trying to walk past them. But it was no use. The school corridor was too narrow and there was no other way out.

"You are such a loser. Your art creation was utterly ridiculous. A baby could have done better" both Dana and Christina sniggered at the same time. "I mean who in their right mind would use real life food for a school project? You definitely should never do anything with your hands ever again. Maybe you should become a shop mannequin. That way you don't need to do anything other than standing in a window and smile with those ugly eyes of yours" they chanted before breaking out in loud and mean laughter. I held on tightly to my school bag. I willed my wobbly legs to just keep on walking. Could this day get any worse?

I hurried past them as quickly as I could. Their laughter ringing louder and louder in my ears. Knowing them, it wouldn't be long until the whole school would hear about it. I made my way down the stairs, across the school playing field and then found my little secluded spot behind our outdoor classroom. It was my hiding place. Tucked away behind some prickly bushes, where I knew I would be left alone. I had fifteen minutes before I needed to get into the hall to have my lunch. Fifteen minutes to make sure that the marble inside my stomach was not going to travel up to my head again. Fifteen minutes during which I just sat with my legs crossed in front of me and contemplated what to do next. Pouring ketchup over the twin's neat and perfectly styled ponytail was one option. But that would undoubtedly get me into even more trouble. Crying my eyes out like a baby was also not really an option. Even though I did give in and let two little silent tears fall down my cheeks.

I had two choices. I could go and tell another teacher how Miss Gosh had treated me. Most teachers in my school were ok. I knew that they would listen to me. But I also knew that someone would then go to Miss Gosh and ask for her side of the story. That was one of my school's thing. There are always two sides to every story. And we get asked all the time to make sure that we hear both sides. I knew that Miss Gosh was going to say that she did not shout at me. And if they would ask someone else, like one of the Princess Twins, whether or not I was telling the truth, I knew that would not turn out in my favour The Princess Twins would innocently declare that Miss Gosh had been firm but very nice to me and only asked me not to use food again. The twins would then flash their biggest and brightest smile, and everyone would believe them. Which means that I would be in even more trouble. Because if they are telling the truth, then I was telling a lie. And if there is one thing I am not, that is a liar. So, option number 2 was to figure out how I could teach Miss Gosh how bad it feels when someone makes fun of you. Maybe that way she would not do that to anyone else again. And with that resolve in my head I felt a little happier.

I made my way to the hall to get my lunch and sat as far away from the rest of my class as possible. All that thinking had made me hungry. Although the Princess Twins were mean about my project, I vowed that I would not let them spoil my lunch.

Chapter 2 - Revenge

It only took a couple of days for my plan to come together. I have to thank my mother for giving me the idea. Usually, my brother Benny and I get dropped off at the school's breakfast club by my lovely dad. Breakfast club opens at 8 am. However, no matter how hard my poor dad tries, we never make it on time. My mum calls him the "biggest fluffer" in the world. I personally think he just has a lot to do in the mornings. And he always needs the loo literally two minutes before we should leave the house. Most mornings with him, it is a case of putting our shoes on, just to take them off again, as dad is sitting on the loo for the next 15 minutes. And by the time our shoes are back on and we have made it to school, breakfast club has already opened. Normally we race through the door, past reception and past the teacher's picture board into the studio. Running in the hope that there is any toast left for us. Not so yesterday. Dad was on a business trip and it was mum who dropped us off. Unlike my dad, my mother did not "fluff". When she was in charge, we were always early. Just like yesterday when we got to breakfast club too early and then spent, what felt like hours, waiting in the corridor for the doors to open. We were so early that none of the other pupils were there yet. Which, for me, was not a problem. I don't mind just standing there and letting my fairy thoughts drift through my deep blue sea of imagination. For my younger brother, though, standing still with nothing to do was not much fun. He didn't like standing still. And as there was nothing to do and nothing to play with, he decided that our mum was going to be his toy. I don't think she liked being jumped on and being pulled at. She was trying to move away from him, which made him even more determined to climb on her. I thought it was quite a funny picture. My mum was moving around in little circles with my brother following her around like a screaming duck. My mum was so distracted by my little brother that she did not see me take out Miss Gosh's picture from the staff picture board. She also did not see that I quickly put it in the back of my school bag. And as my dad was away for three days, we repeated the same game the next day again. You think she would have learnt and left home a little later. But she didn't. She also did not see that I put the picture back into its original place the next day. I also did not tell her that I had made a few copies of Miss Ghosh's picture on our computer at home. I don't think my mum would have appreciated my sense of humour. It was all really easy. The school was still deserted that early in the morning and the minute the breakfast club doors opened, I said that I needed the toilet desperately. And on the way to the toilet, I pinned two copies of my creations of Miss Gosh on the walls. And then I walked back into the breakfast club, picked up my yummy toast and a glass of milk. All I needed to do now was wait.

I didn't need to wait long though.

Just as I was making my way out to the playground at snack time, I noticed that a small group of Year 6 and Year 4 pupils were standing in front of the spot, where I had put one of her pictures. By the time I had walked over, even more pupils had gathered. And most were laughing. Just like I had predicted. I stood at the back and admired my artwork. I didn't make that many changes to her picture, yet my creation looked marvellously different. Her face looked the same. I just added a few bits here and there. Letting my apparent useless hands draw some wild lines around her round face. I drew a small apron on her back and gave her some nice yellow teeth. And then, what I thought was an ingenious idea, I changed her name to Mrs Ghost. I was pleased with myself. The picture did look like a real-life ghost. As I stood there admiring my handywork, my maths teacher Miss King walked past and stopped right next to me. Miss King was one of my favourite teachers. She was kind and funny and always looked happy. When she saw my creation though, her smile disappeared and was replaced by a sad frown.

"Oh Izzy. Isn't that awful? Why would anyone do this? Poor Miss Gosh, she really does not deserve to be treated that way." Miss King said in her sweet and calm voice.

"I know" I uttered back. And in solidarity with her I also shook my head. I was just about to walk back to my classroom, when Miss Gosh turned around the corridor. In her loud and unpleasant voice, she shouted at the crowd. "What are you all staring at. You should be outside for snack time". The other pupils stopped laughing. There was an eerie silence as Miss Gosh ran towards us. I heard Miss King give a big sigh and then she quickly walked in the direction of Miss Gosh, trying to intercept her. But it was no use. She was too late. Miss Gosh had spotted her own picture. She stopped and stared at it. Her face turned a funny colour of purple and red. Her eyes looked as if they were about to pop out. The veins in her neck started getting bigger and bigger. There was going to be trouble. I wondered whether her head was going to explode.

Luckily for me though, I was at the back and without her noticing, I quietly turned around and walked briskly to the outdoor playground. And just as I was about to start climbing on our trim trail, I heard the most incredible and funny shriek that came from inside the school and out of Miss Gosh's mouth. Followed by some rude words that we were not allowed to say ourselves. *Oh dear*, I thought to myself. Someone is going to be in trouble. And this time it would not be me. I smiled to myself. And hoped that Miss Gosh would have learnt her lesson!

Now I just needed to figure out how I could teach the Princess Twins a lesson. Ignoring me was one thing. But to make fun of me and be rude to me was another. That was called bullying. And I learnt from my lovely teacher Miss King that you should always stand up to bullies.

Chapter 3 – The new girl

My art creation of Miss Ghost was the talk of the school for the rest of the day. Even though we were not allowed mobile phones at school, somehow important news likes these spread quickly. There was speculation about who could have drawn the picture. Most pupils in my class reasoned that it must have been the naughty boy in Year 6 that had recently been expelled for a few days. (No one of course knew why, but rumours had it that he trashed his classroom during a break and then did a wee in the middle of the carpet)

I just kept my mouth shut, nodded and smiled. Even the Princess Twins joined in the heated debate, which worked in my favour as my art creation was no longer the focus of their nastiness. They even went as far as claiming to have seen the boy in that corridor shortly before the picture was first spotted. *Such attention seekers, I thought.*

And by Monday lunchtime even the picture was no longer talked about. There was more interesting news that had happened in my class.

Although it was only two weeks until the summer holidays, a new girl joined us that morning. That was totally unusual. Most new pupils join the school at the beginning of a new term. Sometimes in the middle. But I had never heard of anyone joining us right at the end. And neither had my classmates, hence there was a lot of talk going on as to why she was there.

It was a girl named Leila. Which I thought was a pretty name. Our teacher Miss King didn't say much about her. Other than her name and that she would be sitting next to me for the rest of the day. Miss King reminded us to be kind to her and to give her time to settle in. Leila was very shy when she walked into our classroom. Her head was bowed, and her eyes were firmly fixed on the classroom floor. She walked with small, quiet steps and her school bag looked way to heavy on her small back.

Leila looked at me briefly and gave me a little nod, as she took the seat next to me. Apart from that she didn't say anything. Not then and not for the rest of the lesson. I wanted to ask her lots of questions, but there was no time for any chatting. I didn't mind though, as it was maths. Besides, art and DT, it was my favourite subject in the whole, wide world. I love numbers. I love how they add up and never change. Once you knew the number that was it. Not like English. Words constantly changed. At least in my head. Whenever I thought I knew how to spell a word, something funny would happen in my brain and next time I would not be able to remember.

The morning hours flew by and before I knew it, snack time had arrived. By the time I had tidied my side of the desk and found my apple at the bottom of my school bag, Leila was already gone. I walked along the corridor, down the stairs and made my way to my hide-out place behind the outdoor classroom as usual. I pulled the prickly hedge apart and as I was just about to get through the small gap, I let out a gasp. There, sitting in my spot with her legs stretched out in front of her was Leila, the new girl in class.

She looked as shocked as I did.

"Hi" was all I could mutter as I pushed through the gap and sat next to her. To my surprise this little hide-out place was big enough for both of us. Leila smiled at me and carried on eating what looked like red, wrinkly worms out of a tub.

"What is it you are eating?" I asked.

Leila looked up at me with her big brown eyes. She took a deep breath in and then said in a whisper. "These are dried strips of strawberries. My mum makes these for me. They are actually quite nice, even though they look a bit funny". And with that she put a hand in her tub and pulled out a red worm and held it out to me. I didn't want to seem rude, so I took it. I gave it a sniff and had to admit that it did smell like strawberries. I cautiously put it in my mouth and gave it a small chew. To my delight it tasted delicious. Like strawberry ice cream without it being cold and wet.

"They are yummy" I said, and Leila smiled at me. "Anyway, I am Izzy" I said and nodded in Leila's' direction.

"I am Leila. But you knew that already" she responded shyly.

"Nice to meet you Leila. How did you find my secret hiding place?" I asked.

Leila laughed quietly.

"I was a little scared of being in the big playground all by myself. So, I wandered around the outdoor classroom and saw some footprints that led in here. I don't like noisy crowds and I don't know anyone here, yet, to talk to" she whispered.

I felt a little sorry for Leila. It must have been hard being the new girl and not knowing anyone. And I knew how lonely it felt when you don't have friends at the school.

"I know how you feel" I said. "I have been coming here for a few years and most of my classmates are not my friends."

"Oh, why is that" Leila whispered.

"I suppose I am a little different. I like unusual things. And I don't dress like a princess" I said.

"But that is not a bad thing. I like that. I also felt different in my last school. And I don't like dressing in pretty clothes. I prefer to have fun and get messy. Can I be your friend?" Leila asked. This time her whisper sounding a little louder and stronger.

"I would like that very much" I said. "But why are you whispering all the time? I don't think anyone can hear us in here." I asked.

Leila shook her head. "My voice is not very good when I speak. It is easier for me to whisper" she replied.

"Oh. I think you have a lovely voice. But if that is how you speak; I just have to make sure that I clean my ears every morning so that I can hear what you say"

Leila burst out laughing, just as the school bell was ringing again. Well, I say she burst out laughing but really it was just a little shriek. But considering she had only whispered to me for the past 10 minutes, to me it sounded like a big laugh.

We made our way back to our classroom and I sat back at my desk, happy and content. I liked the idea of Leila being my new friend and it felt like learning with her next to me was going to be much more fun.

We met in my secret hide-out place again at lunchtime and Leila told me about her old school and how she was being moved to our school without any real explanation. I told her about the Princess Twins and my complete disaster of an end of year art project, leaving out the bit where Miss Gosh shouted at me. Leila thought my project sounded interesting and unique. She especially liked the idea that I made it look and smell real. Finally, someone understood my creativity!

Chapter 4 - When the words just don't want to come out

I felt sad when Friday afternoon came. Over the past week I had gotten used to Leila sitting next to me and us meeting at every break-time in our hide-out. I never had a best friend in my life before. It felt wonderful to have Leila and to chat to her. When it was just the two of us, she was really funny. I could not understand what could have been the reason for her to have to change schools. It didn't matter though. Her being her at my school was my luck. We hugged tightly as we left school on Friday and I counted the hours until it was Monday again.

Monday morning, I skipped to school, happy to see Leila again and to find out what she had been up to over the past few days. Leila looked as happy to see me as I was happy to see her. She gave me a big hug, as we walked into our music lesson.

Our music teacher Mrs Bart was already waiting for us. I know that is a funny name. It took me several weeks not to laugh whenever someone said her name. And it was even harder to say her name, as my brain wanted to call her Mrs Fart. Thankfully I never said it out loud. I just chuckled to myself whenever the alternative to her name popped into my head. Anyway, getting side- tracked again. Mrs Bart (not Fart, not Fart, not Fart) was the only teacher that sat at her desk when we walked into class and who made us come to her and shake her hand. She looked as old as my granny, but not as old as my art teacher Mrs Gosh. (Ever since I drew that nice picture of her, I have to remind myself not to call her Mrs Ghost. Gosh, my brain is getting tired of all of this thinking). Mrs Bart always spoke with a firm and determined voice. She meant business. She had a funny accent that made her sound like a squeaking bucket at times. Unfortunately, she was not funny at all. Sometimes I wondered whether her and Mrs Gosh were secret friends that would meet up in the evenings and plot how to make school life especially hard for us pupils.

At the start of each lesson Mrs Bart liked to remind us that discipline was the main thing that mattered in life. I didn't agree with that one bit. In my eyes, having fun was the most important thing in life. But that is me, as I often don't agree with what grown-ups say. But I knew that Mrs Bart was not someone that you could mess with. Everyone in the school knew that. She never shouted at anyone, not like Mrs Gosh. She also never raised her hands to any pupils. I think she knew that she would be in trouble if she did. When Mrs Bart became annoyed with anyone, her bushy eyebrows would rise up and big, deep wrinkles would form on her forehead. She would then press her lips together so that only the white tips were still visible. She would shake her head and point her finger at you. And if that happened you knew you would be in trouble. Mrs Bart would make you walk up to her and then she would whisper something in your ear. Well, I say that she would whisper something in your ear. Thankfully, because of my own sweet voice and my angelic smile, I had never been called to her desk. I don't know what she would whisper. All I know is that whoever was at her desk having something spoken in their ear, would then turn bright and, with their shoulders hanging low, walk back to their seats. It would usually only take a couple of seconds for the boy or girl to start crying. No loud tears, of course. Mrs Bart did not like this one bit. They would be silent tears and quiet sobs. Mrs Bart would carry on teaching, ignoring whoever was crying. And the rest of us would try hard to concentrate and not mess up so that no one else would be asked to come to the front. Crying in class was worse than being yelled at!

Thankfully Leila was behind me and she just followed my lead and went up to Mrs Bart to shake her hand. Mrs Bart quietly acknowledged Leila and then, without any comments on her being our new pupil, she moved onto Marcus, who was waiting patiently in line behind us. I sat at my usually spot and Leila sat next to me, giving a little sigh. If I didn't know any better, I could have sworn that she knew what was to come.

Most of the time I didn't mind our music lessons. Even though Mrs Bart was not a happy teacher, she clearly loved music. And so, did I. Last year, we spent two terms learning how to play an instrument. For a lot of my classmates that meant learning how to get a noise out of a clarinet. Playing the clarinet is hard work. Most of the time the only sound we could hear were shrieks or loud air bubbles. Even at the end of year concert, most of my classmates were blowing into the clarinet without much success. I knew how hard playing the clarinet would be and wisely chose to learn the ukulele. Playing the ukulele was easy. It only took me like half an hour to learn "My dog has fleas". Basically, all you needed to do was to strum the ukulele in the tune of that sentence and then repeat it over and over again. I got a little bored and after a few weeks decided to go on to You Tube to learn some more interesting and exciting tunes. This in return, excited Mrs Bart, even though it had absolutely nothing to do with her teaching. I was her star pupil last year. Which meant that I had never been asked to come to her desk for one of her talks. There was a flip side though.

Mrs Bart praising me and showing off her teaching skills on me earned me even more stares and ugly comments from the Princess Twins and her gang of followers. That was nothing new though. I'd rather be left alone by my teacher in class. At least, so far, I had not had one reason to cry in front of my classmates ever. And I was quite good at playing the ukulele by the end of the term.

That was last year though. This year was different. There were no instruments to learn. This year was all about using our own voices as instruments. And no matter how hard I practiced; the sounds that came out of my throat more often than not sounded better in my head than in real life. I wasn't tone deaf or anything. I just wasn't a great singer, no matter how hard I tried. To make matters worse, it was the year of the Princess Twins. Last year both decided to learn the clarinet. Seeing their little, perfect faces falter when they realised that good looks and a smart hair-do alone don't make the clarinet play on its own was priceless. This year though, their polished and good looks were accompanied by angelic voices that always seemed to be in tune. Both were in Mrs Bart's book of favourites. It made my life outside the classroom a little easier as they spent a lot of their time basking in everyone else's praise. Often you would find them practicing another pop song in the playground. Obviously surrounded by their gang of followers who would be glued to their lips and at the end gave a loud and convincing round of applause. Despite that, every so often they would look at me and take it as an opportunity to remind me on how useless my own voice was.

Anyway, I like singing. Just not in front of people in my class. Today though (we had been warned by Mrs Bart last week) was all about showing our understanding of the theory behind the notes. Today, we were going to be tested over what we had learnt throughout the year. Even though this was the last week of the school year, there was no let up. The theory was the boring bit. I wasn't looking forward to this class and counted the minutes until the bell would ring for it to end. After around half an hour of some boring and repetitive discussions regarding which note comes before the High C and what tempo would describe a medium slow piece of music, Mrs Bart stood up from her desk. She must have noticed that we all started to lack enthusiasm and motivation. So, she walked to the front desk, put her hands on it and the said "I can see that you are all looking a little bored. And I know that all you want to do is watch a movie like in all the other classes. But I don't agree with that. School is a place to learn. Even if it is the last music lesson of the year. And to see how much you all know or don't know; I am going to ask two of you to come to the front for a little test"

I could hear everyone take a deep breath in. That was totally unexpected. I looked down at my pencil case and hunched my shoulders, pretending to be invisible, hoping that Mrs Bart wouldn't choose me. I didn't feel prepared and my knowledge of the music theory was patchy to say the least. I don't think I could cope with any more telling offs. Everyone waited. No one made a noise. I could feel Mrs Bart's eyes scanning the room, choosing her victim.

"Christina, please come to the front" Mrs Bart said in her squeaky voice.

Everyone sighed in relief as Christina made her way up to the front of the class. She held her head high and gave Mrs Bart a big smile. She didn't look nervous at all. Mrs Bart asked her the first question, and, without even pausing to think, Christina responded with the right answer. She did the same with the next two questions that she was asked. Mrs Bart was clearly delighted about this. She nodded in full agreement with every right answer Christina gave. And then encouraged all of us to give her a round of applause. Christina walked back to her desk and sat down with a satisfied grin on her face. She was clearly pleased with herself. And I had to admit that I was impressed by her answers. If only she would have not given them in such an arrogant and know-it-all way.

Our class broke into some excited chatter that was rudely interrupted by Mrs Bart clearing her throat and clapping her hands five times. We all looked back at her in silence.

"Well, Christina just gave you a masterclass in what I expect you all to know. But it would not be fair for me just to test one of you, so I am now going to ask someone else to come forward. Before I name one, I am wondering whether there is a volunteer?" Mrs Bart paused and waited for someone to put up their hand. Of course, no one did. I certainly would never raise my hand and volunteer for a test. The chances of failure and being laughed at were too high.

"As no one seems to want to volunteer I would like our new girl Leila to step forward".

My heart stopped for a second. Choosing Leila was even worse than if Mrs Bart would have picked me. Leila had only been with us for just over a week. I looked over to her and saw that she sat with her mouth and her eyes wide open. She looked shocked and totally petrified.

"Come on then Leila. I am sure your previous school taught you the same as we have learnt this year. Anyway, this is a good opportunity for me to see where you are at. Please come to the front" Mrs Bart looked at Leila and I wasn't sure whether she was smiling in support or because she seemed very pleased with her choice. I gently squeezed Leila's cold hand, as she slowly got off her chair. It seemed take her forever to get to the front of the class. Without looking up, she nervously stood in front of us. Her arms were folded tightly in front of her and she was nervously fidgeting with one of the buttons on her grey pinafore dress.

"Leila, the first question I am going to ask you is something easy. You should know the answer to this question. Which tempo is slower – Andante or Adagio?" Mrs Bart asked in her matter of the fact voice.

Come on Leila, just pick one – I thought to myself, willing her on to say something.

Leila shrugged her shoulders and slowly shook her head.

"Leila, you are going to have to make a decision. It is one or the other. It is not that hard" Mrs Bart shrieked impatiently.

Leila just stood there. Her arms still folded in front of her. Her head still bowed down. I could swear she had shrunk by a few inches since Mrs Bart asked her the question. I willed Leila to look into my direction so that I could mouth the answer to her. I kept repeating it silently *Adagio, Adagio, Adagio.* But it was no use. Leila's eyes were fixed on the ground.

"Ok, I take it that you don't know the answer. Let's try a different one."

"What does Calando mean?" Mrs Bart said in a slightly raised and more annoyed voice.

Now that was not fair. Even I didn't know the answer to that. And I was certain that Leila would struggle with that answer too.

Everyone was silent. No one made a noise. Except for Mrs Bart who was breathing hard through her nose. All my classmates were staring at Leila. I silently willed her on to give at least something of an answer instead of standing there in utter silence.

Leila again shrugged her shoulders and shook her head. She was still looking down, but I could see that she had started to tap her right foot on the carpet. Her leg was shaking. Not a lot. But enough for me to see.

Mrs Bart walked over to Leila until she was just a few inches away from her. Mrs Bart leant into her face and said in a quiet voice "Sorry Leila, I didn't catch your answer. Can you please repeat."

Leila flinched as Mrs Bart asked her the question and she again shook her head.

"You are going to have to at least try to give me an answer. And if you don't know then please say so. I think it is rude just to stand there and shake your head. I would expect more from a year 5 pupil" Mrs Bart said in her loud, squeaky, assertive and un-mistakenly no-nonsense voice. I held my breath praying for Leila to give an answer. She didn't know Mrs Bart. She didn't know that saying nothing was even worse than given the wrong answer. I remember David not answering a question last year and Mrs Bart not taking that lightly. He was given tons of extra homework including having to write an essay about why it is rude to ignore teachers.

But again, Leila didn't know that. She was new to the school.

"Leila, did you hear me?" Mrs Bart asked her, this time moving in even closer to Leila's face. Leila flinched again and then nodded her head.

"Leila, I cannot hear you. Do you know the answer to my question or not? I expect you to answer me" Mrs Bart cried.

Leila opened her mouth and I could see that she was trying to give an answer. She took a deep breath and then stuttered "I, I, I d-d-do-o-o-do-no-t know the the a-a-a-". Before finishing her answer Leila stopped and took a deep breath. She tried again, but her stutter this time was even worse. Her face was twitching and by then her arms and hands was shaking. I could hear both Princes Twins giggle behind me. It didn't take long for everyone else to join in. Not me of course. I felt really, really sorry for Leila. She was still standing at the front of the class; her face was bright red and her whole body had started shaking.

Mrs Bart stepped back from her and sat back on her chair.

"That is enough now. Leila does not know the answer. Please sit down again Leila. You have a lot of work to do next year if you don't even know the basics of music theory".

It was only when Leila was sitting down next to me again that Mrs Bart asked everyone to be quiet. And whilst she gave everyone a detailed explanation of the answers that Leila had not given them, Leila just sat next to me with quiet tears streaming down her face. Mrs Bart ignored the fact that the whole class giggled at her stuttering. She also ignored the fact that Leila was crying. This was not fair. My poor friend didn't deserve this.

When the bell finally rang, Leila jumped up from her seat and without looking at me or taking her snack box with her, she ran out of the classroom.

I pulled out a pack of tissues from my bag and walked out to the playground, past the Princess Twins who were standing at the bottom of the stairs.

"Good luck with your stupid stutter-friend. I bet you are glad that you have found someone that can listen to your stupid stories and won't be able to talk back" they chanted as I walked by. Normally, comments like these would have hurt and made me angry and upset. But not today. Today, I was only worried for my new friend.

Chapter 5 – Hugs

I found Leila sitting in our hide-out place. She had pulled her legs up to her chest and was rocking backwards and forwards. She was still crying. Silent tears that were only interrupted by quiet, snotty sobs every now and again.

I sat next to her, passed her a tissue and put my arm around her. After a few minutes of hugging her, Leila had calmed down. Her face was puffy and red. Her eyes were swollen and still watery. But she has stopped crying. Leila blew her nose.

"Thank you" she whispered.

"That is ok. I always carry some because of my hay fever" I said, instantly regretting how stupid that sounded.

Leila blew her nose again.

"That was not nice of Mrs Bart" I said.

Leila shook her head.

"I should be used to it by now" she responded quietly after a while.

"What do you mean?"

"I am not good at speaking up. Especially not when I must speak in front of people. Something happens to my voice and my head. It is like all the words just jump in front of me and my mouth does not want to let them out. And when a sound comes out it sounds nothing like the word I want to say. And the harder I try, the worse it gets. Everyone always laughs at me and that also makes it worse. And now everyone thinks I am stupid. I knew the answers to her questions. I love music. I just don't know what to do when the words don't want to come out of my mouth. I am sorry if I have embarrassed you Izzy. If you don't want to be my friend anymore, then that is ok." Leila whispered.

I looked at her in disbelief.

"Why would I not want to be your friend? You have such a lovely, calm voice when you speak to me. And you are always kind to me. I feel like I can talk to you about anything. I feel sorry for you and the way Mrs Bart has treated you. I think that was totally unfair of her."

"Don't feel sorry for me Izzy. I am used to it. I just needed a little cry and I will be fine"

"But it is not ok" I interrupted. "Mrs Bart should have been nice to you and not put you down in front of everyone."

"Maybe she didn't know that I have a stutter when I speak" Leila said quietly.

"That doesn't matter. She is our teacher and she should be nice to all of us."

"At least she didn't yell at me" Leila responded.

I laughed out loud, remembering my own encounter with Mrs Gosh.

"That is true. Nevertheless, we should plan on what to do about Mrs Bart. We need to teach her a lesson."

"Izzy, can we just leave it? I don't believe in that. My mother always tells me that I should ignore people that are rude to me and not worry about their opinion as it doesn't matter. And maybe it was a good thing that everyone has found out that I stutter. That way I don't have to worry about when everyone is going to find out."

"But" was all I could say before Leila interrupted me.

"I feel better already. I am glad you want to stay my friend. Let's not worry about Mrs Bart or anyone else. Let's talk about what we are going to do during the summer holidays. Have you spoken to your mum about us meeting up?" Leila said, sounding a little more cheerful than a few minutes ago. We spent the rest of our breaktime discussing the summer holidays.

Chapter 6 – Exciting news

Even though Leila felt better by the end of the day, her happiness did not last long. Word of her stuttering had spread throughout our year group and even to some of the Year 6 boys who liked to hang out with the Princess Twins. It seemed that wherever we went at school, someone would make a nasty comment about Leila's stuttering. The Princess twins even invented a new name for her. Stutter nutter. Whispering the name to her whenever she walked past them. And by Friday, this is what a lot of other pupils would call her. Never loudly though and never to her face. And of course, never in front of a teacher. I tried to convince Leila to tell one of the teachers, but she would just shake her head and tell me that it would make matters worse. I think Leila was also worried that she would be asked to leave the school again.

Most of the time Leila pretended not to care. But I knew she found the comments hurtful. Usually, when we walked around the school, she would chat to me quietly. For the rest of the week though, she just walked next to me not saying much. I felt like I needed to do something. Like I did when Mrs Gosh was nasty to me. But every time I mentioned a payback plan to Leila, she would interrupt me and ask me to change the subject.

In the end I decided that all I could do was to be there for my new friend.

We were both excited when the bell rung after snack time on Friday. We only had another hour or so left of the school term before the long summer holidays started. That meant 7 weeks without any bullies and without anyone making fun of us.

We excitedly went back to our classroom where our class teacher Mr Pottom was already waiting for us. Mr Pottom was new to the school and he told us that we were his first class since he had graduated from university. He was a funny teacher, telling us tales from his life before he became a teacher. The first time he introduced himself he asked us to speak to his face and not his bottom, although his name rhymed with bottom. That made everyone laugh. Especially when he then told us that he worked as a bus driver before, spending all his time sitting down. "Now imagine class" he would say "how it sounded when someone would ask me who I am. I would say that I am Mr Pottom who spends all his time sitting on his bottom, driving a bus." Every so often in class, he would tell us about his time driving a big bus that was full of grannies and granddads. And how he felt he was getting older each day by listening to the old people all the time. "So, I decided that I needed to find a job where I work with children. Hoping that this would make me younger" he would say before shaking his head and going through his floppy brown hair pointing out the small grey streaks that had formed at the top of his head. Mr Pottom made learning fun and I was already sad that we would have a new teacher again next term.

Anyway, I am getting quite distracted again. This was our last lesson before the big summer holidays. Mr Pottom greeted us excitedly and then informed us that he had two big announcements to make. Everyone looked at him in anticipation as he picked up a stack of colourful papers from his desk.

"Everyone. Listen! The school has decided that at the beginning of the Autumn term, the school will hold auditions for our own talent show called 'Our school has Talent'. Here is a leaflet, have a look through and consider whether you have any hidden talents. Whether that is singing, dancing or playing an instrument" he said whilst handing out the shiny, glossy leaflets. "And before I forget it, the finals will be held in front of an audience at the town hall and the first prize is a session in a real recording studio in London".

Mr Pottom had just about uttered the last word when the whole class broke out in excited chatter. Well, not everyone. Leila was sitting next to me quietly. She took the leaflet and then pushed it back to the edge of her desk. I glanced at mine and then folded the piece of paper and put it in my bag. Behind us, I could hear the Princess Twins already making plans for what they were going to do on stage. The second I turned around to them (out of pure nosiness), I regretted it. Dana stopped talking and gave me one of her weird, funny looks. The corner of her mouth rose up and her face crinkled as if she had just smelled rotten eggs.

She flicked her long hair back and then leant forward so that I could feel her warm breath on my face. "I bet you and Stutter Nutter Girl are planning some funny act. Maybe you could use your real life stinking moving monster and she could stutter alongside it." She whispered pointing at Leila, who thankfully didn't seem to hear that comment. I was just about to open my mouth to give Dana a piece of my mind, when Mr Pottom interrupted all of us and asked us to be quiet.

"Now class. I can see that you are really, really excited about that. But that is only the first of my two announcements. The next announcement is that I think we don't have enough fun here at school. And you all could do with some more exercise. As a treat I have decided that we are going to spend the rest of our last hour together outside in the sunshine for a game of ultimate tag. Pack your bags, put on your PE trainers and then make your way outside."

We didn't need to be told twice. Everyone hurriedly packed their bags and then ran outside, where we spent the next hour running around like some wild animals having the best time ever. Mr Pottom even joined in, chasing each and every one of us around the playing field. This was possibly the best ending to a school year, ever.

Chapter 7 – Eventually she will give in

When it was pick up time, I was happy that school was finally over. But also sad that I might not see my new best friend every day for the next 7 weeks. Leila was first to leave our classroom. She ran towards her mother and whispered something in her ear, pointing at me. It felt like an hour before it was my turn to finally leave our classroom. My mother was already waiting for me, with my annoying little brother in tow. I hadn't even made it all the way over to her, when my mother gestured to me to hurry up. Thankfully, there were a lot of other excited pupils on the playground so that I only made it over to her just as Leila and her mother got to her. Leila gave me a little wink and I watched intensely as my mother and Leila's mother exchanged what they call pleasantries. I don't really understand that part of being a grown up, yet. What does it matter what the weather is supposed to do tomorrow? And who carers whether the beef was cheaper at Tesco or Sainsbury's this morning. It always seemed to be ages until grown-ups would finally talk about the thing, they wanted to talk about in the first instance. Just like now, both compared how they were feeling, how they were going to struggle in the summer holidays and how hot it was going to be. My brother, being unable to stand still for any length of time, decided to run off onto the playing field. Despite my objections, my mother sent me off to watch and chase him so that she could have a grown-up conversation. I trundled off with Leila in tow and we spent the next 20 minutes playing chase with my brother.

Finally, my mother called over to us.

"Izzy, can you come over here please" she yelled. I picked up my little brother, and half carried him, half pulled him over the playing field to where my mother was standing.

"Leila, I have been chatting to Izzy's mother and we have arranged a few playdates for the two of you. What do you think?"

Both Izzy and I let out an excited shriek, followed by the world's biggest and tightest hug. One for Izzy and one for my mother.

I skipped all the way home. This was the best ending to a school year ever. Not only had I made a new best friend, but I was also going to have lots of fun during the long summer holidays!

The minute we arrived home I bombarded my mother with questions about the actual dates and times I was going to meet Leila. And I repeated my questions every hour. My mother quickly got annoyed with me and tried to distract me by asking me to do lots of things around the house.

"Izzy, go and tidy your room." She said the first time I asked her (just as we had walked through the door). I didn't mind that request one bit. I wanted to tidy my room anyway in case Leila was coming over tomorrow. I finished it in record time and went back to my mother, who was in the utility room folding clothes.

"Oh Izzy, do you have to ask me again? I don't know yet is the answer to your question. Go and put these clothes away". Which I did without a moan or a groan. I needed her to text Leila's mother and not get too mad with me. Our game carried on until it was time for bed. And even then, as my mother was kissing my forehead, I asked her again. This time I knew I had to up my game and asking just once was not going to work.

That was something I learnt at a young age (the other one being nice all the time) was that if I ask often enough, my mother always gives in. I just had to get her to a point where she was really tired of my persistent questioning.

The first time I would ask her a question (like if I could have some ice cream) she would usually say 'no'. Nothing else, just 'no'. The first no from her was almost like a reflex. As if her tongue struggled to form the word yes. After that first no, I would quietly count to ten in my head and then ask in my sweet, innocent 10-year-old voice whether she had changed her mind and I could have an ice cream now. The second no from her was usually followed by a small lecture about why having the ice cream was not a good idea. She would say something like 'it's bad for you' or 'it has too much sugar'. Which obviously is true and correct from a health point of view. But (and there is always a but) – her little lecture gave me the go ahead to start the second part of my mission to extract a 'yes' from her. That is to negotiate and throw arguments at her. Like telling her that I had a sore throat, or that I was really hungry, or that I was really hot. Obviously, none of these were true. I simply love ice cream. The cool and sweet delight would melt deliciously in my mouth. But that was not the point. The point was to keep talking at my mother. Throw arguments at her and wait for her to respond. It didn't matter what she said or how she said it. I knew that the minute she started negotiating with me, I had already won. I don't really get that about adults. I love talking to people and it usually doesn't bother me when people talk to me. Well, sometimes my brother annoys me with his baby language and silly talking. But not to the point that I would get angry or anything. Whereas my mother got more and more irate the more I asked her the same question again and again. It was like a tennis match. She would throw an argument at me like a tennis ball and I would bat it back to her with double strength. It helped that I had a fabulous and quick imagination so that I could always think of my next argument. And eventually my mother would get tired of my questioning and give in with a 'Yes'. Easy as that.

Anyway, here I was with my mother kissing my forehead just before bedtime.

"Mummy, can I see Leila tomorrow" I asked again.

"No" was mother's response. Just like I expected.

"But I really want to see her again, please mummy. Can you not ring Leila's mother and ask whether I can go and see her?" I pleaded.

"Izzy, I am not sure what Leila is up to tomorrow. You can't just ring people and expect them to drop anything. They are probably busy" my mother responded.

"But mummy, what if they are not busy and Leila is as bored as I will be? We could meet and start on a project or something. Like playing music together, or reading books, or playing educational board games."

"Izzy, I think that is a great idea. But I think we should give them a few days before I text her mother and ask her for a playdate"

"Oh mummy, I don't think I can wait that long. You always say that I should see more of my friends. And if I am with Leila you can take Benny to the park and focus just on him" Bang, there it was. Besides my persistent asking I also threw in the fact that my mother could not deny. My brother was as wild as a goose on the playground and my mother usually struggled to keep him under her watch.

My mother paused for a second. I could see the little frown lines on her face as she thought of a possible answer. I just had to use her pause to go in with another comment "Mummy, please, just text Leila's mother and see what she says. That would be amazing. Please, I don't think I can sleep, I am so excited. That would be marvellous. If you text her now she may come back to you before I turn off my light. Oh, I am not sure I could even concentrate on reading. There is so much I need to talk to Leila about" My mother gently placed her warm hand over my mouth. "Sshh now Izzy. I am already dizzy from all your questions. If it means that much to you, I will text her and let you know what her mother says".

'Yes' I thought to myself. I have cracked her again. Now I just had to hope that Leila didn't have any plans for tomorrow. Whilst my mother was back downstairs, I picked up my book and settled on my large, red caterpillar cushion that I had since I was a baby. But no matter how much I tried, I couldn't concentrate on my book. My legs kept wriggling as if they had a mind of their own. I went to the toilet, spent several minutes washing my hands and then went back in my room. I counted until 100 in my head before I decided that I could not wait any longer. I crept past my brother's room and down our narrow, steep stairs to the kitchen, where my parents were having their dinner.

Both looked at me in surprise. I knew I wasn't supposed to be down there. But I just couldn't help it. Just as my mother was getting off the table to walk towards me (no doubt to give me a telling off) her phone beeped. My mother took a breath in and then picked up her phone from the table. I couldn't read her face as she typed in something. I couldn't even be sure that it was Leila's mother texting her. All I could do was hope. After what felt like an eternity, my mother put her phone back on the table. She looked at me and then her face broke out in a massive grin.

"Izzy, your suffering has come to an end. Leila is free tomorrow and I will drive you over to her house at 2pm" I dashed over to my mother and gave her the second big hug of the day.

I was happy. Totally happy. After a kiss on her cheek and a stern reminder that it was now my bedtime, I went back up to my room.

I hopped into bed and snuggled into my yellow, fluffy duvet. I was too excited to sleep and spent the next hour planning on what Leila and I were going to do during the next few weeks.

Chapter 8 – Fun in the sun

It was the first day of our summer holidays and as if by magic today was also the hottest day of the year so far. I fished out my yellow sunflower jump suit that would be ideal for an afternoon of playing in the sunshine.

To my delight, Leila's house was only a five-minute drive away. I made a mental note of the route. Three right turns, two left turns, a few metres along the park, past the small grocery shop and then hers was the fifth house on the right. Leila's house was much bigger than ours. It had two front windows either side of the door. The front door was as big as if it was made for a giant. I spotted an old-fashioned doorbell chain to the right and I eagerly pulled at it, curious as to whether it was working or not. As soon as I had let go of the chain, a concert of several bells echoed in my ears. That was fun and I wished we had such a great invention at our house. As if by magic, a few seconds later the big door opened and a woman with blonde curly locks greeted me. Behind her was Leila, who had the world's biggest grin on her face. The woman introduced herself as Leila's nanny and she asked whether we wanted to come in. I silently hoped that my mother and brother would not come in. This was MY playdate and I didn't want it ruined by my brother being nosy and annoying. To my delight my mother shook her head and murmured something about having some jobs to do. Of course, that was not true. There was no way she was going to get any jobs done with my little brother in tow. Her only job was to get home and then spend the next few hours on the floor with my brother playing pirates and soldiers.

My mother gave me a brief kiss on my forehead before I managed to wriggle out of her arms and ran over to Leila.

"Shall we go in the garden or my room?" she whispered to me.

I shrugged my shoulders and Leila took my hand and guided me along the corridor, through a massive white kitchen into the garden. We walked over the lawn to the back, where Leila led me into a green and purple shed. Well, a shed was a bit of an understatement. The shed was the size of mine and my brother's room combined. It was huge. There was a large sofa on one side, a telly on the wall, a desk and a huge shelf with all sorts of games and books.

"Is this your bedroom? In the back of the garden?" I asked Leila. She gave out a laugh, as she shut the door behind her.

"Of course, not" she said. "This is my garden playroom. Do you like it?"

"It is amazing Leila; you are so lucky. We don't have a playroom. And although I have my own room, my brother usually comes in to annoy me. I would love to have a room like this just for me."

"At least you always have someone to play with. I don't have a brother or sister and it gets pretty boring in here when it is just me" she responded.

"I suppose. But I also think that having a brother is totally overrated. Most of the time he is annoying. He doesn't like the games I like playing. And he gets frustrated easily. You should have seen him this morning. He kept following me around the house with his toy plane and then when I told him to leave me alone, he simply punched me in the back. I tell you what, having a brother is not fun". I said as I sunk into the big brown sofa. Leila sat herself next to me.

"What did your mother say?"

"She was busy cleaning the bathroom and she got annoyed that we disturbed her. My brother is clever. He only hits me when no one is watching. Anyway, he is not here, and we have all afternoon together. What shall we play?"

"Anything you want Izzy. You are the first friend ever to set foot in my playroom and we can do whatever you want" she said.

"I love playing Monopoly. Do you fancy a game?"

"I love playing Monopoly Izzy" Leila chirped. She got off from the sofa and went over to the big shelf, where she picked out the game. She put it on the green rug in front of her and I joined her on the floor.

"Do you know what" I said, suddenly having had a brain wave. "I think we should set up our own club. Just you and me. We could call it the IL girls club, which stands for Izzy and Leila. And if anyone ever wants to join, they have to prove that they are kind and fun."

"I would love to be in a club" Leila shrieked.

And over our game of Monopoly we decided on our own club rules, club logo and club password (which is smelly jelly in case I forget this later).

Leila was great fun to be around with. She had lots of stories to tell and I loved listening to her. Occasionally, her voice would go quiet and a little stutter would come out. I didn't mind that though. I simply waited for her to catch her breath and gave her time to find the right words. The hours at her house flew by. After a round of

Monopoly, we decided to play Tag in her garden and then climbed on a large tree that was right at the back of her garden. At some point her nanny came out with a tray of ice-cold lemonade and chocolate flavoured ice cream. I never wanted this play date to end and sighed deeply when Leila's mother (who had come home only ten minutes ago) called my name from the house, exclaiming that it was time to go.

Leila took my hand and together we walked back into her house to the back door, where my mother was waiting with my little brother.

"Mum, can Izzy come over again tomorrow?" Leila quietly whispered to her mother.

"I am not sure sweetheart. I bet Izzy has lots of other plans for tomorrow and the rest of the holidays." Leila's mother responded. I wasn't sure whether this was a statement or a question. I walked over to my mother, looked up at her with my big, sweet hazel eyes and mouthed a silent "Please"

"Well" my mother responded "as it happens, we don't really have many plans for the rest of the week. I am waiting for a plumber to look at one of our taps tomorrow and I had planned to take the kids food shopping at some point"

"In that case, why doesn't Izzy come over in the morning? I am sure she would have much more fun with Leila. I am so glad that Leila has found a friend and I am sure both girls have a lot that they want to do. And if you like Izzy, you could stay for a sleep-over?"

It took both of us a couple of seconds to fully realise what Leila's mother had just suggested. As if on cue, once we had digested this information, we both jumped up in the air and then started hopping around with sheer delight.

"Well, looks like the girls agree. And I am sure you will have an easier day too, just having to look after Izzy's brother" Leila's mother said, leaning down to my brother and trying to stroke his head. So far, he had been standing there all nice and quietly however the second

Leila's mother touched his hair he started screaming and pulling at my mother's arm.

"Come on Izzy, time to go" my mother said. More like shouted, as my brother's wail was louder than mine or Leila's excited chatter. I quickly ran over to Leila, gave her a hug and then followed my mother to her car.

By the time we turned around the corner my brother had stopped shouting and started bombarding me with what I call "nonsense talk". He started talking about one thing and then another, without any of it really making much sense. There was talk of monsters and superheroes, mixed in with what he had for lunch and what Lego set he was going to put on his Christmas list. He talked at the speed of lightning. Sometimes I wasn't even sure whether he was actually breathing, when he talked like a steam train. Usually, his nonsense talk would annoy me. Today though, after the best playdate ever, I didn't mind. I remembered how sad Leila sounded when she told me that she didn't have anyone to play with. I realised that although I didn't have any friends at school (apart from

Leila of course) I still had a brother. I would never be alone and would always have someone by my side. I made a little mental note to be a little nicer to him and to play with him a little more often. And, as with any good intentions, you should start straight away. Who knows, I may have forgotten this good intention by tomorrow.

When we got home, I offered to run him a bath and then spent the next hour creating bubble monsters on my hand and on my brother's cute little head. And it turned out that it was quite a lot of fun to see and hear him laugh and giggle.

Chapter 9 - Pancakes

I woke early the next morning. The house was still quiet and, although it was already bright and light outside, my clock told me that it was only 6am. My father would get up in half an hour and until then I had to stay in my room. I quietly got out of my bed and tiptoed over to my door, that was wide open. It gave a slight creak as I shut it, however no one seemed to have heard it. I didn't want to waste a single minute of today and pulled out my purple rucksack from under my bed. It was a Christmas present from my grandparents and since they gave it to me it had been sitting under my bed. Today, though, I was going to fill it with everything I needed for my first ever sleep-over. I could feel little butterflies dancing around my stomach just thinking about it. I opened my wardrobe and made a mental list of everything that I would need. I reasoned that as it was summer, I wasn't going to need much. A comfy night dress, spare underwear and a nice dress for tomorrow. I would have to wait a little longer to get my toothbrush, as this was still in the bathroom and I didn't want to risk making too much noise. Next on my mental list was a book. I always had to read before going to sleep. Sometimes I could only manage a page or two before my eye lids would feel too heavy to stay open. Other days I would read for an hour and a finish a whole book. As I wasn't sure how Leila would feel about me borrowing one of her books, I thought I better be safe and packed one of my own. I decided on one of my favourite books ever – Pippi Longstocking. I loved the fact that it was about a small girl with superpowers who lived totally on her own, with only a monkey and horse for company. Her dad was a famous pirate and as he was at sea most of the time, she could do whatever she wanted and whenever she wanted. I imagined how cool that would be. Staying up as late as I want, sleeping as long as I want. Not having to have a bath every day. Being able to eat whatever I wanted. I could see myself surrounded by boxes of pizza, garlic bread and chocolate ice-cream. I knew that would probably never happen. Both my parents were too strict and too much into giving us what they called a clear routine. And pizza was usually something that we got to eat only at other people's houses. But I could dream and reading the book would make me feel as if I was Pippi. I wondered whether Leila had read the book before and whether this was something else we had in common.

Once I had packed my book, I flopped on my soft, grey carpet. The next big question was whether or not I should bring one of my teddies. I still loved being surrounded by cuddly toys at night and had a little, fluffy toy dog that was my favourite. So far, I had never slept a night without him. I wondered though whether Leila will think I was still a baby if I bring my toy dog. I spent the next 10 minutes deciding whether I should leave him at home or bring him along. In the end I decided that I would pack him and decide later whether or not to take him out of my backpack. I put him right at the bottom, where Leila would not be able to see him.

I was rather pleased with myself. It was 6.30am and I was already packed. I heard my father's heavy footsteps as he made his way into the bathroom, followed by the familiar sound of the shower coming on. I picked out some short leggings and a top, got dressed and then put my long hair in a ponytail. I was ready to go and just had to survive the next few hours. I was just about to contemplate what to do next when my little brother bounced into my room.

"Izzy, Izzy, play with me" he shrieked. He was definitely a morning person. The minute he woke up he was full of energy. Normally, I would be annoyed that he came into my room. But considering that I had packed, and I was ready to go, I followed him to his room, where he emptied out his big Lego Duplo box on the floor. We then spent the next few hours building a Lego fortress, Lego ship and battleground – with only a small break whilst we had breakfast and brushed our teeth. To my delight, the hours flew by and it was soon time to go over to Leila's house.

Her mother welcomed us in and whilst my mother made some small talk on the doorstep, Leila took me up to her room, which was on the second floor. She had a whole floor to herself with a bedroom as big as our lounge. She pointed at a large sofa bed in the corner and excitedly acclaimed that we would be sharing this tonight.

I threw myself on the comfy bed and Leila sat herself next to me. "What shall we do today Izzy" she asked.

"Whatever you want. Your house, your rules is what my mother always says" Leila giggled.

"Shall we make a banner for our special IL club"

"That sounds like a great plan. Do you have paint and paper ready?"

"Yep, it's next door in my homework room"

"You have a room just for homework?" I giggled. Leila looked at her feet. She appeared uncomfortable and suddenly very shy.

"I know it is a bit crazy. The room was my parent's idea to help me concentrate better. Do you think that is stupid?"

"Nope, just interesting. I would love to have as much space as you have. Let's go and do our banner" I said as I jumped off the bed again.

Leila led the way to the room next door. Unlike her room, which was filled with lots of pretty things and which looked totally girly, her homework room was white with just a desk in it. Leila opened the cupboard next to it and pulled out paper, paint and paint brushes. She put it neatly on the table and we spent the next hour designing and creating banners for our club. We started off with only two, as it was only us in the club. We shaped it as a flash and coloured it in dark green and blue and yellow. Then we took some thin paint brushes and engraved the badge with our initials. Once we were done, it was already lunchtime and we made our way downstairs, where Leila's mother was in the kitchen. I could already smell the most wonderful smell wafting down the stairs and gasped when I saw the huge stack of pancakes on the kitchen counter.

"I love pancakes" I whispered to Leila. She gave me a big grin, picked up a plate and put three on it for me.

"I thought you might like pancakes Izzy. Wait until you see what my mother has bought for us too" she exclaimed. Leila put my plate on the large table that was nestled in the corner of the kitchen. On it was the probably biggest spread of exciting treats I had ever seen. I spotted chocolate spread, peanut butter, honey, marshmallows, cream, strawberries and salted caramel sauce. Leila went back to where her mother was standing, picked up another plate and pilled four pancakes on it herself.

"Tuck in Izzy" Leila's mother called over. "And help yourself to whatever you want from the table"

I didn't have to be asked twice. I was the Master of building pancake sandwiches.

"Watch this Leila" I said. I picked up the chocolate spread first and put a thick layer on the first pancake. Then I put another pancake on top of that. Then I cut some strawberries in little quarters, halved two marshmallows and put them on pancake number two. Then I covered it with another pancake, some cream and drizzled a tiny bit of sticky honey over it. My stack looked delicious and Leila starred at me with wide, open eyes.

"And now for the best bit" I said. I carefully picked up my sticky, sweet pancake sandwich and took the biggest bite possible. The chocolate sauce had melted a little and was slowly dribbling down my hands. I didn't mind though. This tasted so good. The warm pancakes, sweet chocolate sauce and tangy strawberries tingled on my tongue. Leila laughed out loud and then decided that this looked like too much fun to miss out. She made an even bigger sandwich pancake than me (using four pancakes and adding a cut up banana on top). It hardly stood up and almost fell apart when she tried to pick it up. But, somehow, she managed to lift it onto her mouth and take a massive bite.

After two of my pancake sandwiches, a mouth covered in chocolate sauce and a can of fizzy Fanta, I felt fuller than I had for a long time. My stomach felt like it had rocks in it. Leila and I barely made it upstairs to her room, where we collapsed on the sofa bed, holding our tummies.

"That was by far the greatest lunch I have ever had. Do you always get lunches like that?" I asked.

Leila shook her head "Not usually. I think my mother wanted to impress you. She is a terrible cook usually. And the only thing she is good at are pancakes. So, once in a while she makes them for me. Trust me Izzy. Most of the time she puts a plate of salad and a shop bought sandwich in front of me. Today was definitely treat day" she laughed.

"Well I am glad that I got to experience her only cooking skill she ever mastered. And I will prepare myself for a salad for tonight. Although I feel as if I will never be hungry, ever again"

We both started giggling and imagining what we could make ourselves so that we didn't have to endure a dinner of salad. The more we talked about food, the less we felt we could ever eat anything again.

Chapter 10 – Ukuleles and the best idea ever

Whilst we were goofing around her bed, I spotted a Ukulele bag in the corner of Leila's room.

"I didn't realise you also have a Ukulele" I said. "Are you any good?"

Leila rolled off the sofa bed and crawled along her carpet pretending to be too full to walk. "I love playing the Ukulele. Give me an hour and I will get to it" she giggled. "My mum bought me one a few years ago to help with my stuttering"

"How would using your hands whilst playing an instrument help with your stuttering?" I asked.

"It is a funny thing Izzy. When I play it and sing at the same time, it is as if my brain does not remember that I have a stutter."

"That is weird Leila. Can I see how you do that?"

Leila shrugged her shoulders and finally reached the Ukulele. She sat herself on the floor with her legs crossed in front of her. She didn't move from her spot as she unpacked it out of its shiny, black bag.

"What do you want me to sing?" she asked.

"I don't know. What do you remember? I taught myself to play Somewhere over the Rainbow. Do you know that song?" I said.

"Aww. That is one of my favourites. Promise me that you won't make fun of me though Izzy? I haven't played in front of anyone other than my Ukulele teacher and my mother before" Leila said with a stutter. I could tell that she was nervous, even though she was pretending not to be. And it still surprised me when a little stutter came out of her mouth. Most of the time I had totally forgotten that Leila stuttered. Whenever she spoke to me her voice sounded straight and clear.

Leila carefully positioned her Ukulele in front of her and strummed a few notes before positioning her hands. She then took a deep breath and started playing the song. Her intro was much longer than the one I played, but I liked her version much more. And I nearly fell off her sofa bed when she opened her mouth and started to sing. She wasn't just good at singing, she was amazing. Her voice sounded sweet, yet strong and totally controlled. She sang every note as if she was that little bird trying to fly over the rainbow. I was mesmerised by her singing and it took me a few seconds to find my own voice again once she had finished. Leila looked up at me nervously. She was biting her lower lip. She was waiting for me to say something.

"Leila that was unbelievable" was all that I could mutter.

"I think I need to practise a little more. The last verse sounded a bit off" she said.

"I am not sure what you heard. All I heard was the most incredible signing. You were totally right; you sound different when you sing."

"What do you mean Izzy" Leila asked, her voice etched with worry.

"I mean, and don't take that the wrong way Leila. You have a lovely talking voice, but you always speak quietly, as if you are scared of what might come out. But when you sing your voice sounds strong and just wonderful. Like you mean every word of what you are singing. With that voice you could be a pop star or something."

"Don't be silly Izzy. You are just saying that because you are my friend."

"Trust me Leila, I wouldn't lie to you. Do you know what? You should perform at the school talent show. That would teach everyone a lesson. I mean, if everyone knew what an amazing singer you are, maybe they wouldn't pick on you any longer. Now imagine the look on Mrs Bart's face. That would teach her a lesson or two." I cried excitedly.

Leila just shrugged her shoulders and whispered quietly "Izzy, I could never go on stage on my own. I would rather be picked on for my stuttering than stand on stage all alone. What if no sound comes out of my mouth or so?"

I slowly got off her sofa bed (I couldn't move fast as my belly was still hurting from all the pancakes I had eaten) and shuffled over to where Leila was sitting. I put myself next to her on her fluffy grey carpet and wrapped my arm around her.

"Leila, what if you don't have to go on stage on your own?"

Leila looked at me surprised.

"What if we form a band and we perform together? One of us will get a note out I am sure. I am not the greatest singer, but I love to sing. And even if I sound off key, everyone at the school thinks I am a lunatic anyway after my failed end of year art project. I will be done for anyway, should anyone find out about my little prank on Mrs Gosh. So I don't mind if I make a fool of myself. But I also don't think that would happen. We simply sit on two chairs opposite each other, wear our club badges and pretend to play for us. We just ignore everyone in the room. We pretend to be sitting in your bedroom, just goofing around. We will show everyone what we are made off and that despite all the bullying, we have courage."

We sat in silence for a few seconds whilst Leila was clearly thinking of what I had just proposed. I was pleased with my plan. I wanted everyone to hear how beautiful Leila's voice was.

Leila took another deep breath "What was that thing you said about Mrs Gosh?" Leila said.

"What?"

"You said something about everyone finding out about the prank you played on Mrs Gosh and I don't think you told me about that Izzy."

Daisy poop. Snail porridge. (I always made up funny words when I wanted to swear! That way I manage to stay calm and not let the marble explode in my head with anger)

That tiny, weeny comment must have just slipped out of me. I could pretend that I didn't say it. I could just say that Leila must have misheard me. Or I could do what a good friend would do. Tell the truth, even though I knew this was going to hurt.

"It was nothing really Leila. Mrs Gosh just annoyed me in class last term, so I did a little pay back. You are changing the subject though Leila. We need to talk about our band and our performance during the school's talent show".

I put my hand on Leila's Ukulele and tried to pick it up from her lap. Leila however tightened her grip and gave me a stern look. She looked serious. Very serious.

"You can have my Ukulele once you tell me all about that prank" she said in the sort of matter of fact voice that gave me no choice but to tell the whole story.

I decided to trust Leila and over the next ten minutes explained all about my living art project and Mrs Gosh's unfavourable reaction to it. I tried to keep the bit about her picture short and missed out the bit of having called her Mrs Ghost. But Leila was obviously clever and put one and one together.

"So, you turned her into a ghost Izzy?" she said. I couldn't read her facial expression, and her tone of voice didn't give away whether this was meant as a funny comment or a serious remark.

"I may have done" I stuttered, suddenly very aware of how cruel this all must have sounded to Leila, who could never hurt a fly.

"I was wondering why some of the boys in our class referred to her as the new Mrs Ghost. It didn't make sense back then. I could never see what they meant. In my eyes she looked pretty normal" Leila announced. "But now that you are telling me, I can see why some boys would find this funny"

Leila paused and played a few strings on her Ukulele. I still sat next to her but decided to not say anything for the time being. We didn't speak for the next minute, but that minute felt like an hour.

"The thing is Izzy; I think you are a really nice person. You always seem kind and you have been the best friend I ever had. That is why I cannot understand why you would do something so cruel. I mean, do you have any idea how that could have made Mrs Gosh feel?"

"Not really. I was pretty upset at the time and thought that she deserved it" I mumbled.

"I get that Izzy. But I also know how it feels when people make fun of you. When they twist what you say and then turn it into something that people will laugh about. Maybe Mrs Gosh just had a bad day. Maybe she was stressed. You know how our parents always get stressed?"

"My mother always loses her rag with my brother. But then again - he is a pickle and he does know how to push her buttons" I exclaimed, hoping that we would change the subject.

"Exactly. Now imagine your mother would have had a hard day with your brother and then she had to stand in front of 30 pupils and one of them did something outrageous. Something that she did not expect to happen. Maybe it was never about your living art thing. Maybe Mrs Gosh just had a bad day. Maybe it would have been forgotten the next day. Whereas now everyone calls her by a different name and sniggers when she walks by, which will make her feel even worse"

I had to admit it, Leila had a point. I never thought about what would happen after I put that picture on the wall. I had not even contemplated how it could make Mrs Gosh feel. All I thought about was how it would make ME feel. How it would give me a sense of justice. I felt bad now. Really bad. A small, hard lump formed at the back of my throat. I took a deep breath and thought hard about what to say next.

It was Leila who broke the uncomfortable silence that had formed between us again.

"That is why I never do anything to the people that bully me" she whispered.

"You see Izzy. The bullies make me feel bad about myself. People make fun of the way I talk and stutter, as if there was anything I could do about it, as if their comments would change how I talk. Most of the time it makes my stutter worse. And there was a time when I would have done something about it. One time, this boy who was like a head smaller than me, called me a crazy stutter snake. And every time I opened my mouth, he just pointed at me, stuck out his tongue, hissed like a snake and laughed. After a few times of him doing that I got really angry. You know, the kind of angry where you feel like your head will explode if you don't do anything about it."

"Yes, like you have a marble circling around your head that wants to pop out" I interrupted.

"Exactly. And one day it did. I walked up to the boy, turned my hand into a fist and hit him hard. So hard that my hand hurt like hell afterwards. I was too quick for the boy to react. He tumbled backwards and fell on his back. And because of the way my fist hit his mouth, he lost his two front teeth. The thing was though – I only felt better for like a mini second. Then I saw all the blood and heard how he cried out in pain. I felt guilty and bad. I had hurt another human being. Something I never thought I would do. The worst thing though is that since that day everyone made fun of him. He was after all the boy that lost two teeth by being hit by a girl. I realised then that I had done to him what he had done to me. I made him feel bad. I gave the bullies a reason to pick on him. In the end we both felt bad. People still called me names and laughed whenever my stutter got bad. I had achieved nothing. On the contrary. I felt that I made not only my life worse, but also his.

"But at least that taught him a lesson. I bet he never bothered you again" I said, trying to cheer Leila up.

"You are right Izzy. He didn't bother me again. But others did. There is always someone, no matter where I go. I can't change that. I can't change what people think of me. What I can do though is to never make anyone feel bad about themselves. The bullies will eventually learn. Or at least that is what my mother keeps telling me"

I nodded my head in agreement. That was a lot to think about and it would explain why Leila never fought back when someone in class called her names or made fun of her.

"Anyway Izzy. The problem with Mrs Gosh is that you wanted to teach her a lesson, didn't you?"

"Yes" I replied cautiously.

"How is she supposed to learn a lesson if she doesn't know it was you who drew the picture? I don't think she is clever enough to put one and one together"

I laughed out loud. That was certainly another thing I had not considered. Teaching someone a lesson clearly only works if you tell the person that this is what you want to do.

"You are saying that I should own up to it Leila?"

"Izzy, I can't tell you what you should do. But you should do the right thing. Anyway, enough of this serious talk. Let's put our PJ's on and then practice our song together. Maybe you are right and we should perform at the talent contest at school. Show me what you can play" Leila said as she handed me her Ukulele.

I played my version of the song, not as smooth and sweet as Leila had, but somehow good enough that Leila agreed to my plan to play this song at the talent contest.

We put on our PJ's and spent the next hour quietly practicing our song. We stopped when Leila's mother come up to tell us that it was time for bed.

Once we were snuggled up in bed we chatted about all sorts of things until eventually I couldn't keep my eyes open any longer and I fell asleep.

Chapter 11 – A perfect morning

It was almost 9am when I opened my eyes again. Leila's room was eerily quiet. I couldn't remember the last time I had such a long lie in. Our house was on a main road and when it wasn't the cars that woke me up, it was my little brother bouncing into my room wanting to play. Leila's house however was not on a main road and she did not have an annoying sibling. I turned around quietly in case Leila was still asleep. But she was already awake, smiling at me.

"Do you know that you talk in your sleep Izzy"

"What? I don't remember that" I replied.

"You are actually quite funny in the night. I needed the toilet and when I came back you sat up in bed and spoke about jumping into chocolate and swimming away. I couldn't understand the rest of what you said. And when you were done you lay back down and feel asleep again. First, I thought you were pretending and that it was some weird night-time game you are playing. But when you started snoring and your upper lip wobbled when breathing out, I knew that you were fast asleep again."

"Oh dear. I am sorry Leila. Must have been your mother's pancakes covered in chocolate that I dreamt off last night" I giggled.

"Don't worry, I thought it was quite funny and I fell asleep straight away. Your little snores were like a lullaby. Let's head downstairs and see what delicious feast we can rustle up for breakfast."

We both jumped out of bed and went downstairs into Leila's kitchen. The door to the garden was wide open and a cool breeze came in from the outside. It was a sunny day again. There were no clouds in the sky and the birds were busy chirping away. Leila's mother had set the table outside with a feast of wonderful things. Croissants, chocolate chip cookies, chocolate filled brioche, more Nutella and a big jug of orange juice. This was so unlike my own home, where my mother would usually only allow me to have brown toast with butter and fruit. It was like living in paradise.

"Good morning beautiful girls" her mum called joyfully from the end of the garden. She was kneeling in front of a large green bush, with secateurs in her hand. A big, bulky straw sunhat was resting on her head, trying to block out the sun.

"Help yourself to whatever you want Izzy. Just to let you know that your mother has already texted, and she will come and pick you up at 10am"

I gave a loud sigh. That would give us less than an hour of fun. I gave Leila one of my desperate doggy looks. The sort of look where my eye lids flutter in a desperate attempt to seek sympathy. Leila nodded in my direction and then walked over to her mother. I couldn't make out what she was whispering, but after a few minutes Leila gave me the thumbs up.

She skipped back over to me with the biggest grin on her face. We both sat at the table and I piled my plate high with as much food as possible. My tummy was growling loudly. I wanted to take advantage of all this food, that my mother never bought for me. She did have a point though as nothing on this table was particularly healthy.

"What did you whisper to your mother?" I quizzed Leila.

"I told her about our band and that we want to take part in the school's talent show. My mother thought that this would be a fabulous idea and she agreed that you could come over as much as you want over the next three weeks until we go on holiday"

I jumped off my seat and went over to Leila to give her a big hug.

"That is amazing. I am sure my mother would have no objections to that. I don't think we have anything planned over the next few weeks and we are not going away until the end of the school holidays."

"Excellent. Let's enjoy breakfast and hopefully you will come back this afternoon" Leila chirped.

And this is exactly what we did.

Convincing my mother was easy. By the time she had picked me up at 9.50am (remember, she always had to be early) she looked like she had done a day's worth of work. There were dark rings under her eyes and her hair was standing up in all sorts of directions. She hurried me out of the house and then announced that she had been up all night with my brother. Apparently, he had spent most of the night puking the entire contents of his dinner all over his bedroom floor and then my mother's bed, when he came to wake her up.

Eek. That was the last thing I needed. I hated being ill, especially with a dodgy tummy. I carefully climbed into my mother's car, trying my hardest not to touch anything and gave my brother a stern look.

"Just make sure you stay away from me today" I whispered to him. The second the words left my mouth, he started wailing and screaming.

"Mummy, mummy, mummy" he screeched loudly, making my ears feel like someone was trying to rip them off. I sat back on my seat, my arms folded across my chest. Little brothers were just so annoying.

My mother turned around to face us. Her face was as red as a beetroot. She took a long, noisy breath in and crinkled her nose like she always did when she was annoyed.

"What did you do to your brother?" she barked at me. That was typical. He was the one screaming like a baby and I was getting the blame for it.

"I didn't do anything. I just sat down and then he started screaming for no reason at all."

"As if" my mother responded angrily. "Now shush little one. I know you are not feeling well. Tell me what happened gorgeous". That was another thing that was typical. No matter how ugly my brother looked, or how noisy he was, he was always the little gorgeous one. Why couldn't my own mother see how manipulative, annoying and stupid he was at times?

My brother was still screaming his head off, crying himself into a rage that I knew could carry on for a few hours. My mother turned around, started the car and drove off towards home. He was still crying five minutes later when we pulled up on our drive. My mother opened the car door and gently eased him out of the car. She then picked him up and carried him into the house. I got myself out and shut the car door loudly. But my mother still ignored me. My lovely, happy mood from this morning disappeared as quickly as my mother carried my brother into the lounge. He gave me a cheeky grin as my mother patted his head and told him that he could watch Ninjago's, his favourite TV programme ever. I was ordered to unpack!

I took my overnight bag and went to my room.

I felt a little lost and unsure of what I should do now. Go downstairs and pester my mother to let me go back to Leila's house, or sit here and write a little note to her, telling her that I loved her and that it would be so much easier if she let me go to Leila's. That would pull at her heart strings. Then again, she did look pretty angry with me back in the car. Whilst I contemplated my next move, and therefore my fate over the next few weeks, I heard the faint ringing of my mother's phone. She must have picked it up, as the noise stopped again. I could make out some muffled noises from the kitchen area, followed by heavy footsteps coming towards my door.

I quickly moved to my desk and pulled out a bit of paper and a pen. Better to look like I was doing something educational than just staring into space giving my mother another reason to have a go at me.

Just as I had picked up the pen, my mother bounced into my room. As usual she didn't knock, she just walked in. I wondered at what age I could enforce the "knocking rule". At school the teachers go on and on about privacy. 'Make sure no one sees your privates', 'Make sure you always shut the door when you go to the toilet', 'Always get dressed without anyone watching' blah, blah, blah. That was all very well, however I always wondered whether the teachers had actually been to a child's home before? No matter how many times I tried to talk to my parents and brother about giving me privacy, in my house, that did not exist! I tried putting up a poster on my door, which my brother promptly ripped off. My brother would come into my room whenever he felt like it. My mother would come into the bathroom whether I was sitting on the toilet or not. There was no peace, ever. I envied Leila. She had a whole floor to herself. She had no annoying brother and no one ever barged into her room.

My mother walked over to my desk and put her hand on my shoulder.

"Izzy, I am sorry I shouted at you earlier. I know I shouldn't have done that. You know it is not good to shout. I should have quietly counted to ten in my head. I am sorry, really, but I am just so tired. I am not used to being up most of the night again."

"That is ok mum" I responded. I reckoned that I needed to be nice to her just to make sure that she would not get upset with me again.

"Anyway, that was Leila's mum on the phone. She asked whether you wanted to come back later on. She said something about the two of you planning to take part in the school's talent concert. Is that true?"

I nodded my head quietly in her direction.

"In that case, I would be happy for the two of you to spend the next few weeks together. I have asked Leila's mother to let me know when she is free for practice dates and Leila can come her for some of it. I do think that for the next few days it would be an idea for you to practice at Leila's house though. I really don't want you getting ill as well."

I jumped off my chair and threw my arms around my mother in pure delight.

"I will speak to her again and arrange play dates for the next few weeks. You won't be able to meet every day, as we have some things planned but we will try to fit in as much as possible"

That was good news. Actually, that was more than good news, that was fabulous. The best news ever.

A few hours later I was back at Leila's house, with my ukulele in my hand and the biggest smile on my face.

We spent the next few weeks either at Leila's amazing, fun filled house or occasionally at ours.

It didn't take long for Leila to realise that being at her house had more advantages than disadvantages. It took my little brother an average of only 25 minutes to annoy Leila and to show her that having a sibling was, most of the time, absolutely and totally overrated! Especially since he had taken a liking to her. He would try to get her attention all the time and (because Leila was such a lovely person) she always felt bad about not talking to him. I had learnt that talking to a younger brother often involved rudeness and nonsense. Like the other day when he stood in front of Leila and asked her whether she wanted to hear a song he had made up. She (unsuspectingly) agreed and my brother sang, at the top of his voice: Diarrhoea, diarrhoea sliding out from deep within your bum, like a bullet out of a gun!

You should have seen Leila's face. She didn't know where to look and her face turned as red as a tomato. I had to chuckle to myself. Despite it being a yucky song, my brother did have a little creative streak in him, which I admired. Leila though felt only embarrassment and ever since then never hesitated when I asked to meet at her house. And over the next few weeks we met up as much as we could. The first thing we always did was practice our ukulele duet. Every time we practiced, we sounded better than the time before. Even my singing voice got stronger as the weeks went on. Once our practice was done, we made sure that we had as much fun as possible playing games, running around, getting muddy in the garden and wet in Leila's pool. We spent hours in her little cabin at the back making up stories and playing pretend games. The weeks flew by and if it would have been up to me, I would have wanted the holidays to never end.

Chapter 12 – Stage fright

The new school year started as it always did at the beginning of September. It was still hot and sunny outside, and it felt as if the school holidays were getting shorter each year. I hadn't seen Leila for three weeks by the time the new term started. Her parents took her to Spain for a villa holiday and I went to Cornwall, for a holiday in a lodge. And even though we tried hard to meet up on the last day of the school holidays, our mothers (for once) had other ideas. My feet had grown and as I couldn't fit in my school shoes, she decided to drag us into the nearest town for some shopping. Which I wouldn't have minded so much, but, as it turned out, we didn't just go into a shoe shop. We also went into what felt like every single homeware shop and in a dozen clothes shops. And all my mother ended up buying was a new saucepan. What a waste of a day! When we got home it was already 5pm and my mother decided that it was too late to pop over to my friend's house.

I was mega excited to see Leila gain, even if it meant just a quick catch up in the morning before school started. Leila didn't come to breakfast club, so it was almost 9am when I finally spotted her across the hallway. I walked as fast as I could over to her (we were not allowed to run at school. Another one of those silly rules) and we both fell into each other's arms.

Together we walked into our new classroom, where we were greeted by our new teacher Mrs Monty. She showed us our new seats and to my delight, Leila was sitting right next to me.

The bell rang and just as Mrs Monty was about to shut the door, the Princess Twins walked in. Everyone in the room fell silent and turned around to face the door. There they were, walking into class as if it was a fashion show. Both curled their plump rosy lips, showing off the lipstick they were wearing. Both with identical hair styles – a bun right on top of their heads, that made them look much taller than they actually were. Both clutching new school bags, which were decorated with sparkly, diamond like stones. And to top it all, both wearing school shoes with heels. I watched how the other girls reacted to this sight. Most sat with their mouths open, staring and nodding, just what the Princess Twins wanted. They took the last two seats in class. Thankfully, on the opposite side of the classroom from me. At least this year there were not going to be any more comments directed at us from behind.

"All right now everyone. Listen" Mrs Monty said clapping her hand five times. Everyone turned around to face her. Everyone, except for the Princess Twins who had their heads together and were giggling quietly.

"Dana and Christina. I am pleased that you managed to join us at the last minute. I do suggest however, that if you have anything to say, you say it out loud or leave my classroom and discuss it outside" Mrs Monty said in a firm voice, looking at the Princess Twins. Both straightened up and looked at her. I quietly tapped Leila's hand and smiled at her.

"And also" Mrs Monty carried on "May I remind everyone that, although you are the oldest in the school now and Year 6 is the stepping stone to secondary school, the same school rules apply to everyone in here, as they do to our new reception children. That means no make-up or lipstick, no fancy hair do's and certainly no school shoes with heels. And I expect everyone at their desk at 9am sharp. I can see that some of you have forgotten those rules and for today, I will make an exception. Should any of you however ignore those rules, then there will be a direct consequence from tomorrow onwards. If you chose not to be in class by 9am, I will lock the door from the inside, and you will have to spend the school day helping out the caretaker. If you chose to not conform to our uniform or hair policy, you will be taken to the medical room, where I will personally oversee that our office staff find some second-hand clothes from the uniform shed for you to wear. I may want to remind you that we are usually very short on donations for larger clothes and that you may end up wearing a uniform that is too small. And lastly, should your school shoes have a heel, you will be required to take them off and wear a pair of the spare green Wellingtons I always keep in the caretaker's hutch for a rainy day. Again, I may remind you though that I will not check for any spiders or insects before asking you to put these on."

There was a loud gasp spreading through the classroom. And both Princess Twins turned bright red. They looked like they had swallowed a beetroot. I tried hard to suppress the loud giggle that wanted come out of my mouth. Thankfully, everyone else was trying to do the same! Mrs Monty gave all of us a few seconds before resuming her class. Leila and I liked her very much. She was outspoken and matter of the fact, and clearly didn't take any nonsense from anyone, especially not from the Princess Twins who still believed they ruled the world.

Obviously, they didn't like her one bit. Mrs Monty's speech was the talk of the day. The Princess Twins acclaiming that they would continue doing what they wanted and that they wouldn't let any teacher tell them what to wear. Funnily enough though, both came to school with new shoes, a simple ponytail and no make-up the next day. Unfortunately, although they looked more normal and less like dolls, their attitude and behaviour were still the same as last year. Leila and I tried to stick together as much as we could. We avoided the Princess Twins whenever possible and spent most of our break times at the opposite side of the playground or in our little hideout place behind the outdoor classroom. That turned out to be more uncomfortable than we remembered. We both seemed to have grown over the past few weeks and suddenly, the hedge branches were scratching our heads and shoulders.

It didn't matter though. Since the summer I no longer felt the need to be on my own. And Leila was confident enough to chat away to me even though other people were around

After only three days, we got used to the new school routine. The lessons were harder than last year and the homework longer. We still had to read every night and aim to finish a book per week. We almost had no time to just goof around and everyone was expected to take on new jobs around the school. Leila and I both chose to help out at the library twice a week after lunch, which was fun and meant that we could chat to each other a little more.

And we had loads to talk about.

The main subjects were the upcoming auditions. I handed in our reply slip first thing Monday morning and received our invitation to audition by Wednesday. The auditions were to take place the following Monday, straight after lunch. We only had one more weekend to practice before then. Our playing sounded pretty good and Leila's voice was still amazing. The one thing we had not thought about though was what we were going to wear or how we were going to get on stage (silly things like whether we should carry our Ukulele's on our right or left hand).

By Monday morning though, we had it all figured out. I would walk on stage first and Leila would simply follow my lead. Even though we knew the words to our song off by heart, I had printed off two copies of them in large print. You never know what those nerves would do to us once we were on stage. The auditions started at 2pm and we were asked to meet in the studio 20 minutes beforehand to warm up, change or do whatever we needed to do to prepare for our act.

We spent our lunchbreak doing a last-minute rehearsal and then made our way through the school into the studio.

We both gasped when we walked in. The studio was full! The shrill noises from all the other pupils were hurting my ears. The room smelled like old trainers, just ten times worse. Everywhere I looked people were moving or dancing around.

I knew that the talent show was going to be a major event, but I had not expected that many pupils to audition. There were only 15 slots available. I did a quick count and stopped at 50! That meant that we only had a slim chance of even making it through. Leila sensed my concerns and she pulled me towards the far corner of the room.

"Izzy, I can't believe how many there are. And look at them. They are all glammed up. Look at the fancy costumes some of them are wearing. Look over there, some are wearing pointe shoes and full ballet outfits" Leila whispered, whilst pointing at a group of Year 5 girls who were indeed wearing pointe shoes.

"Don't worry about it Leila. Let's just do our thing. You never know what the judges will be looking for. Maybe those girls are not even any good in those shoes. I always thought you had to be in Year 6 to go on pointe. But then again, I don't know much about dancing. It is something that has never interested me before" I said, trying to cheer Leila up.

Just as we were getting our Ukuleles out of the bag, I heard an all too familiar snigger and laugh.

"Now look at what the cat has brought in" Christina shouted at Dana, who was standing only a few metres away from us. With all the noise and pupils in the hall I had not realised that we put ourselves literally next to the Princess Twins. Both were dressed in a tight black gym outfit. They had a red belt tied around their tummies and were wearing bright red dancing shoes. And I was sure that I could smell perfume on them. As if that would impress the judges.

Dana frowned. First at Leila and then at me. "They look as rough as if they have just fallen out of bed" she exclaimed.

"And look, they are going to play an instrument. You will look like the lady and the tramp with that. You could have at least tried to brush your hair. But I suppose that would be too much hard work" she said, pointing at me.

Christina burst out laughing. "Let's just hope that stutter girl doesn't try to open her mouth as well as playing the squeaking Ukulele" she said loud enough for everyone around us to hear.

I swallowed hard. Maybe it was just my imagination but suddenly, I felt that everyone stopped talking and was staring at Leila and me. As if the show had already started and we were the first act on stage.

I felt myself getting hot, angry and upset, but just as I was about to say something equally nasty to the Princess Twins, I felt Leila's hand gently tugging at my arm.

"Leave them Izzy. Remember it won't make you feel better" she whispered in my ear. "They are not worth it."

I contemplated whether or not I should still say something, but before I could utter a reply, Dana shouted across to us "Did she say anything? Why don't you ask her to speak up so that we can all hear what she has to say? I bet all that comes out of that mouth is rubbish gibbering though" she laughed. Christina laughed too and to make matters worse stuck her tongue out as if she was going to be sick.

I put my arm around Leila and stuck up my middle finger to the Princess Twins. Thankfully, before anything else could happen, I heard the voice of Mrs Monty across the room.

"The next Act to audition is the 'Sparkling Diamonds'. Dana and Christina to the studio please"

If I hadn't been so upset and angry, I would have laughed. They called themselves 'Sparkling Diamonds'. Diamonds are supposed to be pure, clear and beautiful. A better name for them would have been 'Rotten Eggs'. They look alright on the outside but once you get to the inside they are just rotten. Just like Dana and Christina's personalities.

Both hurried towards the door, confident and with their heels clicking heavy on the wooden floor.

It was only when they had left the room that I looked at Leila. Her face was as white as a sheet and I could make out sweat pearls on her forehead. I felt so sorry for her. She was the kindest person in the room and certainly did not deserve to be treated that way. If only other people could see that.

"Are you ok?" I asked her cautiously.

Leila nodded her head quietly. I could tell that she was trying her best not to cry.

"I think I just need to pop to the loo quickly to wash my face Izzy" she said.

"Do you want me to come with you?"

"No, I think I will be fine. Just give me a second. I need to be on my own otherwise I will just end up crying" Leila whispered and then made her way through the crowd.

I watched her walking to the door, her back hunched over as if she was carrying a crate of rocks.

I took a deep breath and started unpacking my Ukulele. I needed to focus and concentrate if we wanted to have any chance of getting through these auditions.

"Don't worry about them" I heard a voice saying in my direction. I ignored it. Surely that was not meant to be for me.

"Izzy. Are you ok? I mean, really, don't worry about them. They are just jealous!"

What the caterpillar?? was the first thing that popped into my head. Not only was this voice talking to me, but it also said something about the Princess Twin's being jealous of me? Who was that talking to me? I slowly looked up, halfway expecting to have imagined this. But no, standing right there, right in front of me was my classmate Thomas clutching a silver flute.

"Oh" was all I could muster.

Thomas had been my classmate for the past three years. I had never taken much notice of him. He was quiet and tended to keep himself to himself. He was friends with Ruben, who was equally quiet. Last year Thomas sat at the same Maths table as me and we spoke about numbers, equations and mathematical things. But we never spoke about anything other than maths. Yet, here he was, standing in front of me being nice.

I tried to compose myself. I straightened my back, trying to look totally not bothered or surprised.

"Why would they be jealous of me?" I asked Thomas. Well, it wasn't really asking him, it was more like demanding him to tell me. It was the most ridiculous thing I had heard since my failed art project. Why would the Princess Twins, who had everything, be jealous of me? They always wore nice clothes, their parents lived in big houses, they could afford to have their hair done at a proper hair salon and most of all they had a ton of friends that thought the sun was shining out of their bottoms.

Thomas moved a little closer to me. Close enough that no one would have been able to hear what he had to say. I could smell some aftershave on him, which totally surprised me, as I always thought that boys our age didn't care about things like that.

"Because you know who you are. You don't try to impress anyone. And it doesn't matter what you do, you always do what you think is right" he whispered.

I was certain I could see him blush as he uttered these words. Which was a good thing, as I could also feel my cheeks burning. I tried to think of a clever answer, or anything half-way intelligent to say to him. I looked at his face and noticed how he had changed over the past months. He looked older, more grown up and his eyes seemed to have gotten darker than I remembered. And he certainly smelled good!

"Thank you for this" was however the only thing that eventually came out of my mouth.

"You are welcome. And Good Luck. I am sure you will be amazing" Thomas said, just as I heard the strong and loud voice of Mrs Monty calling us in.

Chapter 13 – The auditions

"Izzy and Leila to their audition, please" she called.

Leaking water bottle and smelly cat. Our audition.
Suddenly, I didn't feel prepared any longer. And where
was Leila? Why had she not come back from the toilets?
Panic rose in my chest. It doesn't happen a lot – but I did
not know what to do. I slowly walked over to Mrs
Monty. Clutching my Ukulele in my right hand and the
song sheet in my left. Just like I had practiced at home. I
walked as slow as I could, hoping that the extra seconds
would be enough for Leila to make her way over here in
time. But she didn't come back into the studio by the
time I got to Mrs Monty. Or when I walked through the
wooden door that led to the hall. Mrs Monty walked
back to the table that was positioned right in the centre of
the hall. Next to her, our head teacher Mrs Horn was still
writing some notes. And next to her was the head of our

PFA Mrs Tree. Mrs Tree gave me a welcoming nod with her head and gestured to me to come closer.

Mrs Horn finally looked up from her piece of paper.

"Hello Izzy" she chirped. "We were expecting Leila to audition with you. Are you no longer performing together?" Mrs Horn asked me.

I shifted from one foot to the other. I had two choices, again. Lie or tell the truth. If Leila would have been standing here, she would have told me to tell the truth. Tell the head teacher that Leila had been bullied by two of her classmates. That she ran out of the studio and not come back, yet.

But what good would that do? No one, I mean really no one, would believe us. The Princess Twins would twist what they had said. And everyone else around us would be too scared to admit to the truth. They were all too scared that it would be them next time.

I took a deep breath and slowly counted until 5 in my head. Today was not the day for the whole truth. It was also not the day to lie. Those times were over. I had made a pinkie promise to Leila never to lie again. I decided just to let out a few details of the actual truth.

"Yes, it is Leila and me that had planned to perform together. We had planned to play a duet on our Ukuleles. Unfortunately, just a few minutes ago, Leila became unwell and she said that she had to go to the toilet. Maybe it was something she had eaten at lunchtime. I don't know." I said with my head held up high. I was pleased with myself that it sounded totally like I was telling the truth.

Mrs Horn wrinkled her nose like she always did when she was thinking.

"Ok Izzy, that is a shame. We have another hour of auditions to do and will have no time to listen to both of you later on. And I fear that Leila will not be feeling much better later. So, why don't you show us what you can do, on your own, and we will decide based on your performance. If it is good enough to go through, then I am sure it would be even better with Leila playing by

your side at the Talent Show. And if it is not good
enough, then you simply must try again next year. Tell
Leila to bring a packed lunch next year so that she
doesn't come down with a dodgy tummy again" Mrs
Horn said with a twinkle in her eye.

"Right then Izzy. Show us what you have for us" Mrs
Monty chirped.

I walked over to the only chair that was close to the panel
and sat myself down. It meant that all three had to turn
slightly to see me perform. But I didn't care. I had no
spare hand to move it and anyway, it wasn't about the
way I looked. It was all about playing a beautiful song on
a beautiful instrument.

I counted until three I my head and then started
strumming my Ukulele. My hands felt nervous and for
the first few cords, my left hand felt rigid and cold, as if it
didn't belong to me. But then, almost as if my muscles
remembered the song, my hands just played on their
own. I took a deep breath, opened my mouth and started
the song at exactly the right point. First only humming,

then singing the first line "Somewhere over the rainbow, way up high". And whilst singing the song and playing along I thought about what it would take for Leila to ever walk to the end of the rainbow, to a magical land where no one would ever make fun of her and where everyone could hear what a beautiful voice she had. A land where we didn't need to hide behind bushes at lunchtime just because we were different.

And whilst I was thinking those thoughts, my hands kept playing and my voice kept singing. I didn't need to look at the song sheet that I had carefully positioned by my shoes. I remembered all the words and all the cords with ease. It was only when I got to the end of the song that I finally looked up at the three people that sat at the table. They all were smiling and nodding.

"Izzy, that was beautiful. Thank you for sharing the song with us" the head teacher Mrs Horn said calmly.

"Thank you" I said. I got off from my chair, picked up my song sheet and walked out of the hall. With my head held high. Because I felt totally proud of myself.

If only Leila could have been there.

Our next class had already started, and I made my way back to our classroom. I expected to see Leila sitting at her usual chair. But it was empty. There was no sign or trace of her.

Mr Pottom was our teacher for the rest of the afternoon. I wanted to ask him whether he knew where Leila had gone or whether anyone had noticed that she was missing. I decided not to though. The Princess Twins were sitting on their seats, still in their outfits and completely dolled up. I simply didn't want to give them any more reason to be mean today.

It was only another hour until the bell finally rang. I grabbed my school bag and ran down the stairs as fast as I could. The Princess Twins were too busy telling everyone about their amazing audition that they didn't notice me passing them.

My mother was waiting for me in the playground like she does most days. I looked around her, to the spot where Leila's mother or nanny usually waited for her. I couldn't see either of them and sighed with relief. That meant Leila had gone home where she was safe from any more bullying.

My mother bombarded me with questions about the auditions and I couldn't bring myself to tell her exactly what happened. I simply smiled, gave her my biggest toothy grin and told her that it was great. I then offered to retrieve my brother from the trim trail, to make sure we were leaving the school grounds as quickly as possible.

We were home within 7 minutes, a record for my brother. I told him that I wanted to play an exciting game with him, and he fell straight into my trap. I simply told him that I was pretending to be a dinosaur and he had to ran away from me, as otherwise I would eat him up. He was so easily persuaded and giggled all the way home.

The minute we arrived home I threw my school bag into the hallway and then told my mother that I had promised Leila to pop over to go over our audition. My mother didn't question me. Probably because we had spent so much time together during the summer holidays.

I ran all the way to Leila's house and impatiently knocked on her big front door. No answer. I knocked again, this time harder and louder.

It felt like ages before I heard footsteps and the big front door creaked open.

Leila's mother looked at me surprised.

"Hello Izzy. Sorry I was on the phone. Why didn't you ring the doorbell?" she said. "Can I help you?"

"I am here to see Leila. I want to make sure she is ok" I panted, still feeling breathless from my run over to her house.

"I am sure that Leila would appreciate that, but you know that she has complaint of a sore tummy and I don't want you to catch anything" she responded, sounding concerned.

"I think I will be ok. It must have been the chicken at lunchtime" I responded. Again, not a lie, just an opinion.

"Ok then. Come on in. Leila is in her room. You know the way" her mother said. I walked past her, uttering a quick 'Thank you' and walked up the stairs to Leila's room.

Her door was shut. I gently knocked on it until I heard a faint voice asking me to come in.

Chapter 14 – Caring and forgiving

I found Leila lying on her bed, face down. She was still in her grey and green school uniform. Apart from her tie that had been thrown across the room and that was hanging half off her sofa bed. Leila lifted her head up just enough to check who had come into her room. I could make out her big, hazel eyes that were red and swollen. The minute she saw me, she buried her head back into her large bed pillow. Leila started crying again. Not the little cries she did at school, No. These were big tears, with big sobs and sighs. I could make out her tiny chest rising up and down with every heavy breath she took.

I could feel my own tears collecting in the corner of my eyes. I gave my head a gentle shake. Now was not the time to cry. My friend, who probably thought that the world had ended, needed me to not weep like a willow.

I walked over to her bed and sat next to her. I wasn't sure what I needed to do next. I never had a best friend, and I never had to really comfort a friend before. Back in our secret hideout I always put my hand on Leila's when she got upset. I couldn't do that now. It didn't seem enough this time. And (which didn't help) she was lying face down on her hands. It took me a while to consider my options.

Lie next to her. Pat her back. Pat her shoulders. Stroke her hair. Do nothing. Just sit there.

In the end I decided to give her back a little stroke. It took Leila a few more minutes until her loud sobs were replaced by the quiet sort of tears that I had gotten used to from her. Eventually, she lifted her head up from her wet pillow and carefully sat up next to her. She made a big snort and then wiped her nose on her school cardigan, leaving a little trail of snot.

"I didn't think you would ever come and talk to me again" Leila said. Well, she didn't say it that way. It took her three attempts to get the word 'think' out and then another five attempts to get the word 'talk' out of her mouth. This was one of the worst stutters I had heard from her, ever. I just sat next to her and looked at her, giving her all the time in the world to get the words out she needed and wanted to say.

"Why wouldn't I want to come and talk to you again?" I responded quietly.

Leila sobbed again. This time only for about a minute or so.

"I, I, I, I let you down. I didn't think you wanted to be my friend anymore" she stuttered once she had calmed down a little.

"You didn't let me down, honestly. I was just worried about you when you didn't come back into the studio. And I was even more worried when I couldn't find you later."

Leila let out a big sigh. And then she threw her arms around me and gave me a big, crushing hug.

"You are the best friend I have ever had" she said, this time with a little less stuttering.

"So are you. Just promise me that you will tell me next time you are leaving the school without me" I said.

"I won't do that again, I promise Izzy. I now realise that this was a stupid thing to do. I just felt so upset and angry about what the Princess Twins said to me in front of all the other pupils. Then I was worried that all the teachers would laugh at me for stuttering on stage"

"They were all really nice" I said with a big grin.

"What? Did you audition on your own? How was it? How did you do?"

"It was great Leila. We will find out tomorrow if we made it"

"What do you mean 'we' made it? I wasn't there, this was all your doing!"

"We are team, remember Leila. This is a performance for two. We are the IL club. I told them that you ate something dodgy at lunch and that you didn't feel well. So, if we get through you will be on stage with me in two weeks' time showing the world what we can do!"

Leila gave me another big hug "Izzy, you are amazing. Thank you!" And I had to admit it, making Leila feel good again felt amazing. Much better than showing off my moving art monster! Or seeing the angry face of Mrs Gosh looking at a scribbling of her face that I had turned into a ghost.

Chapter 15 - Results

I knew that the results of the auditions had been made by the screams and jubilant cries I heard the minute I walked out of our classroom after the first lesson of the day. I took Leila's hand and gave it a big squeeze. This was it. The moment of truth. We made our way downstairs and waited for the big crowd of pupils to move away from the notice board. The results were printed on a single piece of white paper. Too small to read unless you stood right in front of it. Our view was obscured by two big, bouncy heads that had long ponytails bopping up and down. Of course, it was the Princess Twins. It felt like wherever we were these days, both were not far away.

"Yes" both exclaimed throwing their fists in the air as if they had just won a fight.

"I mean, that wasn't really a surprise, was it Dana?" Christina asked. Well, it didn't sound much like a question. It was more like a well-known and well researched statement. I wondered where they always got their confidence from.

"No, of course not. We were amazing. Our routine was just what they were looking for" Dana said, trying to put on her poshest accent. *As if anyone was going to fall for that,* I thought.

Both turned around at the same time, almost hitting me and Leila with their flailing arms.

"Now look who is here. Stutter girl and her useless smelly friend" Christina said whilst eying me up and down. I wondered why she needed to do that, especially since we had already spent the last hour and a bit in class together. That surely would have been enough time for her to check out what I looked like today. (Not that I looked any different than any other day. A ponytail and green hairband was still my preferred hairstyle)

"Watch your dirty mouth. Or like my grandmother always says 'Don't say anything if you have nothing nice to say'" came from a deep voice behind me. I quickly turned around to see Thomas standing behind me. Had he just tried to defend me and Leila?

"Whatever" Dana replied to him, boldly and defiantly flicking her hair. She took Christina's hand, barged past us and walked down the corridor. I had expected them to give Thomas a piece of their mind. Instead, they gave him an evil glare and just walked away.

"Did you get through?" Thomas asked me before I could think of anything to say to him.

"Ahm, I am not sure, yet. We haven't looked" I said.

Thomas, who was already around a head taller, leant forward and then stood on his tip toes to look at the piece of paper. There were still around five other pupils blocking mine and Leila's view, but with his long legs Thomas was able to look over all of them.

"Yep, there you are. Just as I thought. Izzy and Leila."

"Oh, my snotty handkerchief" I said.

Thomas laughed out loud, "Handkerchief? I don't think I have heard that word since we studied Romeo and Juliet last year" he cried.

I shrugged my shoulders and then turned over to Leila. I didn't have time for this banter. Me and my friend had just learnt that we made it to the live performances for our school's talent show. Leila put her arm around my shoulders "Well done Izzy, I am so proud of you" she whispered.

"Yep, well done Izzy" Thomas said, even though I didn't think he heard what Leila had said to me. I gave him a shy smile and nod and then walked outside with Leila to the back of the school field. There was, once again, lots to talk about. And lots to plan. Especially how I could make sure that my friend wasn't going to run away again.

In all my excitement about this pending huge event, I forgot to ask Thomas whether him and his flute also made it through.

Chapter 16 – The final is finally here

If there was anyone at the school who hadn't heard about the upcoming talent, that person must have been blind, deaf and away with the fairies. Once the finalists had been announced, it was as if a big machine had been turned on. Out of nowhere (or possibly out of the PFA cupboard) big banners appeared all over the school. Colourful, shiny leaflets lined the front desk and were placed in everyone's school bag. Posters were put up all over the school. Even the door to the staff room was covered in posters about the talent contest. Emails were sent out to all parents daily (I know that because my mother moaned about the flurry of activity in her yahoo inbox every night) promising an evening of 'Unforgettable performances, fun, prosecco and chocolates' (which even my mother had to admit was very tempting).

And, as if by magic, all the acts that made it through were treated like royalty. First, we were asked for an important meeting with our headmistress and the head of the PFA. Usually, that would have been a rather scary undertaking. You only went to the head of the school if you had done something terribly wrong or if you had done something exceedingly wonderful, neither of which ever fell into my kind of 'being a child' category. I was neither terribly misbehaved nor was I ever wonderfully clever'. We met out headmistress and she declared that from now on we would be excused from class for half an hour every day so that we could perfect our act. I thought that was a great idea, especially since we were all given a rota and had the exclusive use of the upstairs music room. Leila thought that was a great idea too and because we could practice every day, she was becoming more excited about our performance.

You could even say that the next week was an almost perfect school week, and we would have forgotten all the nasty comments from the Princess Twins. If it wouldn't have been for the two of them trying to outdo everyone else. From the moment they walked into the classroom to the moment they went home – the talent contest was all they talked about. And when I say it was all they talked about I am telling the truth. I could probably have coped with that, considering we were all excited about it. Dana and Christina and their "Sparkling Diamonds" group as they called it had to go further than that though. Somehow, they managed to produce their own leaflet that they handed out to anyone they passed. A sparkling piece of pink paper, covered in silver glitter, with a picture of them in their little dance outfits. And written across was 'Vote for the best dance group ever. The Sparkling Diamonds". I mean, really? Either they missed a point, or I did. The voting was done by a chosen panel of grown-ups. Even though it was called "Our school has got talent" like the big show on ITV, there was no phone in. I simply could not see the point in them having produced their own leaflet.

I looked at it, folded it in my pocket and then threw it in the next bin. But that was not all they did. They had to practice every free minute they had. In the corridor in-between lessons, in the outdoor classroom at lunchtime and right bang in the middle of the field at pick up. They didn't just dance either. They got as many of their so-called friends to gather around them and sing the main tune to their routine. It felt like wherever I looked, I could either hear or see them.

Leila wasn't half as bothered about it as I was. She was more worried about how much practice they got in that we didn't. And she was worried that they might win the whole contest.

"Izzy look" she would say and point at them "Dana is doing a supported handstand whilst Christina is doing the splits. That is some real talent". I just shrugged my shoulders.

"Leila, anyone could do this. And look how out of tune they are with the music. Just don't pay any notice and focus on our performance" I would say, not wanting to admit that I was a little (and really only a little) worried about their competition.

"Anyway, maybe them two are not the ones to beat Leila"

Leila looked at me, surprised and a little puzzled.

"Why? Have you seen any of the other acts?"

"No, of course not. Maybe that is not absolutely the truth", I stuttered

"Izzy you are cracking me up. Since when do you stutter? That is my thing!" Leila said quietly whilst holding her hand over her mouth, pretending not to laugh. "What do you mean though?" she asked once she managed to keep a straight face again.

"As you know from our meeting with the head, Thomas got through too. And I met him outside the music room the other day when I needed the loo and he asked me whether I wanted to hear him play the flute"

"Isn't the music room on the first floor and the toilets on the ground floor Izzy?"

I could feel my head getting hot and my cheeks burning. I don't even know why, all of a sudden, I felt totally shy and insecure. I took a deep breath, trying to compose myself.

"Okay, he asked me during one of the breaks whether I wanted to hear him play and we made a plan that I would ask to go to the loo during maths and then sneak upstairs to hear him. I just wanted to support him. He has been nice to us after all. You know, he doesn't have many friends and I think he wanted someone with musical talents to hear him play"

Leila laughed out loud (which she doesn't do a lot. Although I couldn't really see why my comment would have been THAT funny).

"And anyway Leila" I responded "He was very good. I got tiny Goosebumps when he played. So maybe he is the one we need to watch out for"

Leila just stood there, nodding her head. I think she wanted to say something but decided to keep her thoughts to herself for once.

Before we all knew it, the day of the finale had arrived. We managed a last-minute rehearsal session after school and agreed to meet outside the town hall at 6pm. The show would start at 6.30pm and we were not expected to be called on stage until 7.30pm. We were given the order of the performance that morning and, to no surprise to us, our slot was straight after the Princess Twins and just before Thomas, who was the last act of the night.

It didn't take me long to get ready. I had a shower and washed my hair. We decided that it was sensible not to have any hair tickling our faces, so I put mine in a straightforward and simple ponytail. Leila said that she would do the same. I picked up some black leggings and a black top, attached my IL club badge and that was me done. Leila and I decided to keep thing simple. Our act was not about glittery outfits, funky hairstyles and a face covered in make-up. Our group act was about playing a beautiful song on a wonderfully sounding instrument.

We arrived at the town hall at 5.45pm. That was even despite my dad (the notorious mega fluffer) coming along. Crowds of people gathered outside the hall. There was a buzz in the air as if it was the premiere of an important film. Wherever l looked I saw people, teachers and fellow pupils. Mr Pottom waved at me enthusiastically from the double doors at the entrance. Somehow, everyone was really excited about tonight. Leila, her mum and dad arrived shortly after us. I sighed a massive sigh of relief. She was here. In flesh and blood. I wouldn't have to be on that stage on my own. We gave each other a quick hug and then left our families and sneaked in at the back, like we were told to do.

The back of the town hall was also bustling with noise and tension. Even though there were less people here than during the auditions, somehow the noise was even worse. We were greeted happily by Mrs Monty, who ticked us off her notepad. She took us to the back of the room and went through tonight' order of appearance again.

"So, I will call you up to the back of the stage around ten minutes before your turn. You will then wait behind the stage, where you can watch the act before you. Let me just check, yes, that is Dana and Christina and their 'Sparkling Diamonds' dance routine. Once they come off stage, the head of the PFA Mrs Tree will announce your act. Just to double check – you don't have any backing tracks or any special requests, do you?" she asked us.

"Nope, just us" I responded, with Leila nodding her head in agreement next to me.

"Right then, there is a buffet over there. Help yourself but don't overdo it on the sweets. We don't want you getting tummy ache again" Mrs Monty said in Leila's direction. Leila again nodded her head quietly.

"Ok then, I will leave you to it. Good luck you two and well done for making it to the final" Mrs Monty exclaimed before turning around and walking over to Thomas, who had also just arrived.

Leila, Thomas and I spent the next hour practicing, talking and watching the other acts. Everyone else decided to get some last-minute rehearsals in. We were happy with our acts and enjoyed the buffet food and lemonade. I reasoned that another few minutes of practicing would not make us any better than what we already were.

One by one the other pupils were called to the stage until only a few of us were left. Unfortunately, that included the Princess Twins, who we had been able to ignore until then. I had hoped that with Thomas sitting by us they would leave us alone and not make any nasty remarks. I should have known better.

First both just started pointing at us and giggling. Then Dana started making some sort of gestures. I had no idea what she was trying to say, but I was sure that it wasn't anything nice.

I could sense that Leila was getting more and more worried. She clenched her ukulele hard and tapped her shoe anxiously on the floor. Just like she did during Mrs Bream's music tests.

"I am not sure I can do this Izzy" she whispered to me. "My tummy hurts and look - my hands are shaking. Maybe us performing was all just a bad idea! What if I start stuttering? What if I don't manage to get any words out?"

I gently put my arm around her. "Don't worry, ignore them. You know what they are like. We are going to do this. There are a lot of people watching us that are looking forward to it. The Princess Twins are just two people that we really should not care about. Even if you don't manage to get a word out, I will. It is not about winning. It is about being here and doing something that takes bravery and guts."

Leila took a deep breath in. "Okay" she whispered half-heartedly.

"Let me get you another one of these chocolate brownies. That will take your mind of things" I responded, just as Mrs Monty called the "Sparking Diamonds" (aka the Princess Twins) to come up for their performance.

Dana and Christina got up from their chairs and walked towards Mrs Monty as if they were on a catwalk. They seemed to have decided to change their outfits last minute. Gone were the black leggings and tops. Both were wearing sparkling high heels, silver glittering miniskirts and sparkling tops that were not long enough to cover their belly buttons. Their hair was scraped back into a tight (and rather uncomfortable) looking ponytail that was covered in glitter spray. Both wore bright, red lipsticks and I could swear that their eye lashes looked longer than they did this morning. If I didn't know them, I probably would have not recognised them. Everything about them looked weird. Out of place and not right.

They walked slowly. I presume so as not to fall over in their big heels. I have often wondered how anyone manages to walk in shoes with a heel the size of a brick.

Just as I thought they were done with hurling insults at us, Christina looked me straight into the eye and with a funny grunt in her voice chanted "I wish you two stuttering scarecrows all the luck in the world. I think you will need it".

I couldn't believe her cheek. Wasn't it enough that poor Leila was already feeling down and sad? Why did they always have to hurt her more even though she never did anything to anybody?

I could sense that Leila was close to giving up. By now, I had come to know her pretty well. She didn't cry or anything, but I could see that her lips were pressed together lightly, and a little frown line appeared just above her lovely, brown eyes. And I knew that she was upset, as she just stopped talking!

I contemplated what to do next, but before my little brain came up with any sort of sensible and happy conclusion, Mrs Monty walked back into the room.

"Izzy and Leila please. You are next" she called from the other side of the room. That was probably a blessing, as we could do nothing else but follow her to the back of the stage, where our destiny was waiting for us.

Chapter 17 – This is it

I simply took Leila's hand and pulled her off her chair. Well, I had to use a little more force than just pull her. I dragged her off her chair and she reluctantly followed me to the back of the stage. She clutched her ukulele and for a second I thought she was going to break it. Mrs Monty chatted away to us, oblivious to what had just happened. I didn't hear a word she was saying. All I could think of was that I had to somehow get Leila up on stage with me. Giving up was not an option. I didn't want to have to find her lying on her bed again, feeling upset and sorry that she had let people down.

I knew that she could do it. I had heard her sing many of times by now. And I genuinely believed that she had the most amazing voice I had ever heard. I needed for everyone to hear that. She deserved it. She deserved for people to hear how wonderful she was. That the stutter was just a small part of her. But that it was by no means a reason for anyone not to hear her. I felt it was almost my mission to show all those people that had been cruel to her in the past that they were in the wrong.

Leila grudgingly followed me, and we reached the stage just as the Princess Twins were gliding onto the stage in their sparkling outfits and high heels. A huge round of applause greeted them.

I put my arm around Leila again, giving her a hug and a squeeze. Holding on to her. That way, there was no chance of her running away. I gave her a small kiss on the cheek followed by a quiet well-done. I wasn't sure whether she heard me, as in that precise moment, the music for the 'Sparkling Diamonds' dance act started blaring out.

The Princess Twins were crouched on their knees when the music started. They bobbed their heads in the rhythm of the beat. They slowly lifted their heads, their hair sparkling and their costumes glittering in the bright stage light. The music got faster, and both rose up from their positions, dancing and jumping to the tune. So far, they were not bad. I had to admit it, they actually looked good. The next bit of their routine was for Dana to do a handstand and for Christina to stand behind her, holding her legs up. I watched as Dana lunged forward. She put her hands on the stage floor. She threw her legs in the air. And she fell flat on her face. Christina had stumbled in her heels and didn't catch the legs.

A huge gasp went through the audience as Dana landed on her back with a massive thump. Christina managed to catch herself. She just stood there, watching her friend fall over.

Dana let out a nervous shriek as she scrambled up from the floor. She didn't look hurt. Just annoyed. She gave Christina an evil glare and both carried on dancing. There was a small cheer from the audience, as both resumed their routine. Most people though, like me, held their breaths, wondering what was to come.

And what came was not good. Both were totally out of sync with the music. Dana stepped on Christina's toes when she was supposed to walk backwards. Christina turned right when Dana turned left. Their miniskirts kept riding up their bum cheeks and both kept trying to pull them down. Whatever it was they were doing; it was no longer and well-rehearsed dance act. More like two lost chicken, flapping and jumping up and down running away from a fox.

This was turning into a disaster for the 'Sparkling Diamonds'.

The music was still going when a little laughter started at the back of the audience. And with every wrong step and desperate look on their faces, the laughter got louder and spread further towards the front of the stage. People were laughing at the Princess Twins, not because they were trying to be funny, but because their whole dance routine turned into a farce.

Their music had not even finished when both decide to run off stage.

I could see tears in their eyes. Small, but visible rivers of mascara were rolling down their cheeks, they were crying. The one thing I thought was not possible, Dana and Christina were crying.

Not for long though. The minute they reached the back of the stage they started fighting with each other. Mrs Monty rushed towards them and tried to usher them off the backstage area.

I looked at Leila, who had a big grin on her face.

"Serves them right" she said in a strong and determined voice.

"Leila, we are supposed to be nice people" I said, but really only meaning it half-heartedly.

This was, after all, a contest and we had just watched two of the lead contenders having an epic meltdown.

Having seen the Princess Twins clearly losing the plot seemed to have spurred Leila on.

The chair of the PFA Mrs Tree took to the stage and before we knew it, called out our names.

I took Leila's hand and gave her a positive nod. This time she nodded back at me with a smile. This was it. This was our time.

We walked over to the two wooden chairs that were placed right into the middle of the stage. Leila sat down first and positioned her Ukulele on her lap. I gently pulled the microphone a little further down to her side, ensuring that she would be heard even at the back of the hall.

We were facing each other. I glanced over to the end of the stage. The light was so bright that I couldn't make out anyone in the audience. It felt as if we were in Leila's bedroom. Just the two of us, playing a song together.

I took a deep breath and looked at Leila. She had her ukulele firmly in her arm. Her right hand was on the right strings. She was ready. And so was I.

I quietly counted – one, two, three and started strumming the first few cords.

Leila was supposed to be joining in at the third cord.

She didn't.

I repeated the cords again.

And she still didn't join in. Leila sat at on her chair. Her fingers were not moving. She looked like a statue.

I repeated the cords again, pretending that this is what we had planned all along.

My brain was working overtime. I had to do something. Anything.

I repeated the cord again and then leant into the microphone.

"Ladies and gentlemen. I now give you the wonderful Leila"

And then I repeated the chord again. This time, though, Leila's eyelids flickered, and her left hand started moving. Firstly, really quietly, then a little stronger and by the time I had repeated the chord twice, she had caught up with me.

I took a deep breath in, nodded in her direction and then started humming the first line of the song. Just like we practiced all those times in her room.

And when it was time for Leila to start singing, she did.

She sang the first few words softly "Somewhere over the rainbow, way up high and the dreams that you dream of, once in a lullaby". I joined in, quieter than her, strumming my ukulele in the calming and sweet tune of the song.

Leila just kept singing. Her voice getting stronger. Like she was that little blue bird trying to fly over the rainbow. The room was so quiet that you could have heard a penny drop. The only sound you could hear were our two ukuleles playing in perfect harmony. And Leila's amazing, angelic voice. There was no stuttering. There was no whispering. Just her singing like she had never sung before. I kept my voice low; this was not about me.

And although I had heard her sing this song many times before, the little hairs on my arms stood up. I had forgotten that we were on a stage. I had forgotten that around 300 people were watching us. I was with Leila, in the land where dreams do come true.

Chapter 18 – We did it!

I finished playing a few notes before Leila. I watched as she gently strummed her ukulele for the last time.

And then there was silence.

I gave Leila one of my big smiles. Not a fake one like I gave Mrs Gosh after she shouted at me.

I gave Leila a 'Well done, look at you' smile. The sort of smile best friends give each other.

My best friend had just taught everyone in the room the biggest lesson ever. Inside, she had the most amazing voice and you just needed to be quiet and listen to her to hear it.

We both got up from our chairs. It didn't matter what anyone else thought. We had done our best. Even winning this contest didn't matter anymore.

Having been up here and having given our best was all that counted.

Within a few seconds though, the room exploded. There was clapping, chanting, whistling and shrieking. People called our names. It was hard to make out what people were saying. I could only hear snippets like 'that was amazing', 'wonderful', 'incredible', 'we want more'.

This time it was Leila who walked over to me and took my hand. She edged me forward to the front of the stage and then bowed down. I followed her lead, albeit with my mouth open the whole time.

We bowed twice more before the chair of the PFA Mrs Tree came back on stage to announce the next act. Thomas had already walked on stage when we finally made our way back. Once we were out of side Leila threw her arms around me.

"Izzy, that was by far the most amazing thing I have ever done. Thank you for making me do this. Thank you for believing in me" she said. And for the first time ever, Leila didn't whisper this to me. She told me. Loudly. With no stutter.

"It was indeed" was all I could say.

We were reminded by Mrs Monty to keep our voices down. And although I was full of excitement (my hands were still shaking from the buzz I felt back on stage), I signalled Leila to be quiet and pointed at Thomas, who had just started playing his flute.

We watched as his hands glided effortlessly across his flute. I had no idea what song he was playing, but in my eyes (and ears) it was beautiful. The audience thought so too, as his applause was as loud and cheerful as ours had been.

Thomas bowed several times before the chair of the PFA Mrs Tree walked back on stage to announce a 20-minute break before the results would be announced.

I could hear that the room erupted in excited chatter the second the curtain had been drawn. Chairs scrapped on the wooden floor and people chatted noisily. If only we had seen all the acts so that we could have had an idea of who may be the winner.

"Alright everyone. Can I please ask all the acts to sit and wait behind the curtain? If you need a wee now, please take your place first so that the people next to know how much of a space to leave. Please sit in the order of your performances. That means Year 1 children start at the left of the stage and Year 4 children start forming a new line behind the little ones." Mrs Monty announced. Slowly, all the other acts came back from behind the stage area. It took several minutes for everyone to find the right place. Leila and I sat down next to Thomas. I had just about wondered where the Princess Twins were, when I saw two hunched over girls in sparkling outfits slowly waving through the smaller children to the gap that we left to our right. Both sat down, this time not looking at anybody. Their faces looked red and puffy and I could swear that both still had tears in their eyes. Their mascara was smudged and there was a slight lipstick mark across their faces, where they had tried to wipe their mouths. I nudged Leila to get her to look at both, however I shouldn't have bothered as she was already staring at them. I had expected her to laugh (or at least smile) but the expression on her face was stone blank.

Without saying a word Leila got up and walked into the direction of the toilets. I was too stunned to say anything. It was hard for me not to break out in laughter. I glanced over to Thomas who must have read my mind, as he also looked like he was about to burst into laughter. I shrugged my shoulders in his direction and he gave me the thumbs up, not that I have any clue what he was trying to tell me. After only about a second, Leila came back and sat down next to me, this time on my other side though. She turned around to Dana and Christina and it was only then that I noticed a large supply of toilet paper in her hand.

"Don't worry girls. You did your best and that is all that matters. Here, I have brought you some tissues so that you can wipe your faces. There is a bit of your lovely mascara that needs to be wiped off." Leila said in her sweet voice. There was no stuttering and no pausing. She genuinely meant what she had said. Both looked at her open mouthed. Dana did a big sigh and then picked up some paper and started wiping under her eyes. Christina hesitated for a second before she also took some tissues. Leila gave them some gentle instructions as to where their faces were marked, and both followed her advice without batting an eyelid. Once their faces were clean, Leila took the used tissues, got up and put them in the bin next to the stage. She took her seat again and gave me a nod.

"Thank you" was all Christina mustered to say, followed by Dana saying the same.

We spent the next few minutes sitting in silence. I didn't think it was right to make a joke and somehow this little act of kindness made me think. After all the nasty things the Princess Twins had said to Leila, after all the times they bullied her, she still wanted to help them and be nice. She could have easily made fun of them, as their faces certainly looked like that of a scarecrow, and yet she didn't. She stayed true to herself. And I had to admit that I was in awe of her strength and determination to being good. I promised myself that from now on, I was also going to be a kinder person.

Just as I was about to tell Leila how proud I was of her, a tall man walked up the stage, holding a golden envelope. He was followed by our head teacher Mrs Horn.

Everyone fell quiet as the curtains opened again. It took a few seconds for my eyes to adjust to the sudden brightness and I had to blink several times. This was it. This was the moment of truth.

Mrs Horn turned on the microphone and asked everyone in the room to be quiet.

"Ladies and Gentlemen. This has been the most exciting talent contest I have ever been to. All the children did extremely well. I was truly proud of everyone that showed us their hidden talents. Can I ask everyone for another big round of applause for all the finalists again? Finalists, please can you stand up, and enjoy this applause. That is just for you"

We all got up and I held Leila's hand as we savoured the loud and cheerful clapping of hands.

"Thank you very much. I will now pass the microphone over to Mr Cowly, who is one of the producers of the 'Funtastic recording studio' in London. He was part of the judging panel and I understand that they have reached an undisputed verdict"

Mrs Horn passed on the microphone to Mr Cowly, who nodded excitedly.

"Hello friends. Hello finalists. Can I first of all tell you how impressed I was with everyone who performed tonight. Even though there were some mishaps I hope that all of you remember that it took bravery and strength to come up on stage and perform in front of everyone." Mr Cowly paused as another round of applause spread through the room once again.

If we carry on like this, we will still be here tomorrow – I thought to myself.

"After only a short debate, we have finally reached a decision. Can I have some drum rolls please" he said and as if by magic, a loud drum roll noise came out from the loudspeakers.

"In third place and therefore having won a Karaoke machine each are……. 'The Splendid Singers'. Can I ask Marie, Susan, Maggie and Aneesh from Year 3 to step forward to collect their award!". Another huge round of applause and excited cheers came from the audience, as the girls jumped forward to collect their award from Mrs Horn.

I squeezed Leila's hand harder. Maybe, with any luck, we have made it to second place, I thought.

"In second place and therefore having won a family ticket to Thorpe Park is…… Thomas and his flute from Year 6".

I looked over to Thomas and gave him a thumbs up. He looked shocked and surprised at the same time. He slowly made his way to the front of the stage where he accepted his award from Mrs Horn.

This time, Leila squeezed my hand. "Don't forget Leila. It doesn't matter that we haven't won. We performed and that is all that mattered" I whispered to her. Leila gave me a smile and nodded her head in agreement.

"And now ladies and gentlemen. The moment we have all been waiting for. Before I announce the winner of tonight's talent contest, I want to say a few words about why we have chosen that act. The wining act tonight impressed us with a stunning performance. A performance that did not need fancy lighting or make-up. There were no acrobatic jumps involved. No glittering costumes. Just two girls, who played and sung beautifully and who showed us that with friends, anything is possible. I am honoured to announce that tonight's winners of a recording session in my studio in London are……. Izzy and Leila and their Ukuleles"

Oh, my chocolate covered apple. Did he really just say it was us? I looked at Leila, whose face had turned a grey sort of ashen. I jumped up in the air and gave her a massive hug.

"Leila, we did it. Can you believe it?" I shouted in her ears, hoping she would hear me through the explosion of noise in the hall.

I took Leila's hand and together we walked up to the front of the stage where Mr Cowly handed us a gold covered microphone statue. We bowed down to a thunder of applause and looked over to the audience who were on their feet, clapping and cheering us on.

I can't really remember what happened next. I had never been so excited, happy and nervous in my life before. This was the first time ever that something like this had happened to me. I vaguely remember talking to Mr Cowly and then shaking what felt like a hundred hands. It was only when I went back outside, where the cold crisp autumn air blew through my hot head, that I felt vaguely like myself again.

Both our parents were waiting for us and we embraced them with happiness and pride.

It was my dad who made the first move and went over to Leila's parents.

"Well, that was certainly a surprise, wasn't it" he said to Leila's dad.

"I think that calls for a little celebration. Would you like to come back to our house for some nibbles and drinks? I am sure the girls have loads to talk about and it would be a shame to end this evening now" my dad announced.

Leila's parents looked at each other and then both nodded in agreement. "That would be great. Thank you for the invite"

Leila gave me another squeeze and just as we were about to set off, I could spot two solemn figures approach us. It was Dana and Christina. Both were wrapped up in their coats, hiding their glittering outfits. Both shifted uncomfortably, as they stopped in front of us.

"Erm, we, erm, you know, well what we wanted to say" Christina stuttered, which was totally unlike her.

"What we wanted to say" Dana interrupted "Was that you both did really well. You have amazing voices and we just wanted to say Congratulations. And that we are sorry that we said some mean things to you."

I couldn't believe my eyes or ears. The Princess Twins stood in front of us apologising. Telling us that we did well. No insults, no nastiness. That was a surprise.

It was Leila, who broke the silence. "Thank you very much. And we accept your apology" she said. I was just about to open my mouth, when I could feel her elbow slightly digging into my side. Leila looked at me and I knew that I needed to keep my big mouth shut for once.

The Princess Twins nodded quietly and then turned around.

"I really wanted to give them some of my mind" I protested.

"I know" Leila said. "But what would that do? Let's just be happy for today. It must have taken a lot for them to come and say this to us. I'd rather be friends with them than continue having to avoid them. After all, you can never have enough friends, can you?" Leila chirped. "And if there is one thing we need to debate over – it is how you are going to apologise to Miss Gosh about that horrid picture of her you put up in the corridor Izzy"

Daisy poop, she hadn't forgotten. I laughed out loud and agreed that I would maybe, but only maybe, consider tomorrow what I could do about it.

Tonight, there were more important things to talk about. Winning the shiny trophy, planning our trip to the recording studio in London, and if we had a little more time later on (and only if no one else was listening in) then we needed to talk about Thomas, who had asked ME whether I wanted to be his girlfriend.

Tonight, was certainly by far the most exciting and amazing night of my life, EVER!!!

Printed in Poland
by Amazon Fulfillment
Poland Sp. z o.o., Wrocław

54454871R00106